Medical Malpractice
A Preventive Approach

Medical Malpractice
A Preventive Approach

William O. Robertson, M.D.

UNIVERSITY OF WASHINGTON PRESS
Seattle and London

Library of Congress Cataloging-in-Publication Data
Robertson, William O.
  Medical malpractice.

  Bibliography: p.
  Includes index.
  1. Physicians—Malpractice—Washington (State)
2. Medical jurisprudence—Washington (State) 3. Medical
laws and legislation—Washington (State) I. Title.
[DNLM: 1. Financial Management—methods. 2. Malpractice.
W 44 R652m]
KFW326.3.R63 1984   346.79703'32   84-40322
ISBN 0-205-96162-7   347.9706332

Contents

Preface

Chance plays a pivotal role in our lives, and so it did with the origin of this volume. As virtually the only non-lawyer among multiple relatives—father, brother, uncles—I brought with me an interest in the philosophy and concepts underlying the legal field as I entered medicine. Joining the Dean's Office at the University of Washington in 1963, I was fortunate to participate in decentralizing the medical education program throughout the sister states of Washington, Alaska, Montana, and Idaho (known as WAMI). It was clear to me and to others involved in developing the program that providing appropriate liability coverage for students and malpractice insurance for residents and faculty located in the WAMI region was a major requirement for the initiation of the program and its eventual success. When its description was published in the *Journal of Medical Education* in 1971, as far as I can determine it was the first in the medical education literature dealing with the issue of medical malpractice.

Again, chance proved pivotal in 1975–76. As the "malpractice crisis" reached its zenith, I was serving as the president of the Washington State Medical Association (WSMA). That year the issue consumed most of WSMA's energies and much of its budget. I concluded then, and still conclude, that the best remedy available to the malpractice problem is prevention.

Subsequently, the WSMA has mounted a prevention program aimed at changing physician behavior and enhancing public understanding of the issues involved. Towards that end, it has sponsored a "Risk Management Program," with education as an essential ingredient. The first step involved gathering data about the epidemiology and the causes of the crisis. Then it initiated a series of symposia and seminars across the state; subsequently it arranged to publish a "Malpractice Case of the Month" for serial appearance in the "WSMA Reports" section of the Association's official publication, the *Western Journal of Medicine* (1980–84). I accepted the task of writing the series which now involves more than eighty cases.

This volume is a compilation from that series of case reports and an expansion of their setting. For the most part the cases are derived from actual experience in the state of Washington and many have been modified slightly to maintain anonymity. Each section includes, in addition to the case(s), a review of the medical and legal issues at hand, together with suggestions and recommendations about avoiding specific problems in the future. These suggestions, in portions of the book titled "What You Can Do," are intended to assist physicians and others responsible for the Quality Assurance Program in hospitals, clinics, and offices in carrying out their tasks.

I am grateful to many individuals for their help in the preparation of the series and this volume, particularly John Arveson, Jean Knights, Bill Weil, Diane Wade, Ann Staberg, and Jeff Smith. Special thanks are due my physician wife, Barbara Robertson, for her contribution of ideas, patience, and attention to communication details. I hope the book will prove informative and useful in contributing a medical perspective on the costly and acrimonious problem of medical malpractice.

Medical Malpractice
A Preventive Approach

1

Introduction

Case Report. W. B., a 25-year-old male, was admitted to the hospital via the emergency room for head and associated injuries received in an automobile accident. His blood alcohol was in excess of 0.2 percent. Skull x-rays revealed a non-depressed 2 to 3 cm fracture in the left parietal area; spine films were interpreted as normal. No localizing neurological signs were present, but the patient was combative, hyperactive, and "abusive to staff."

The patient was observed in the intensive care unit and sedated with paraldehyde, but remained disturbed. Approximately 20 hours after admission, ICU attendants noted that he was no longer moving his legs. It was later determined that he had sustained a fracture of a high thoracic vertebra which caused bleeding into or around the cord. He was left with significant permanent disability.

A number of factors, including failure to diagnose, entered into the lawsuit that followed W. B.'s treatment. But perhaps more importantly, the family reportedly overheard employees in the ICU calling the patient a "ne'er do well," "junkie," and "alcoholic," and criticizing the attending physician's participation in the patient's care. The family claimed that the operating neurosurgeon and staff at another hospital, where definitive procedures in a case of this type were carried out, had also criticized the handling of W. B.'s case.

In addition, it was brought out in litigation that the original order sheet in the patient's chart had been altered by the addition of an order to "keep patient flat," an order which the nursing staff uniformly agreed had not been present at the time of hospitalization.

This multi-problem case resulted in a sizeable financial settlement for malpractice.

Ninety percent of all malpractice suits ever filed in the United States have been filed in the past two decades, a mere 3 percent of the nation's existence. Over 90 percent of all dollar awards and settlements were made in the same period.

In medical annals, 1975–76 will go down as the "year of the malpractice crisis." The combination of rapidly escalating premiums, burgeoning lawsuits, large financial awards, and difficulty in obtaining liability insurance threatened both the individual physician and the medical profession as a whole across the country. And the consequences, in turn, threatened the delivery of medical services to patients. One of the greatest challenges facing the medical profession today is maintaining the highest standards of medical care at a time when cost containment has become a national goal. Moreover, defensive medicine is advocated too often in an effort to reduce the tremendous financial losses from malpractice litigation—losses which are passed on in medical costs to an often hostile public not inclined to accept error in this age of technology-intensive medicine.

The response of doctors to the crisis was predictable. Committees and task forces studied the questions of liability, seeking hard-to-retrieve data and easy-to-obtain opinions about the sources of and potential solutions to the malpractice threat. As might have been expected, the profession rapidly indicted: (a) the legal system, unscrupulous lawyers, and contingency-fee arrangements; (b) the insurance industry and its pricing and accounting practices, plus what some physicians see as its "obscene profit margins"; (c) unfair laws passed by attorney-dominated legislatures; (d) the jury system for blatant breaches of fairness and justice; and (e) patients and their families anxious to strike it rich by taking advantage of a bad medical outcome that was not necessarily produced by negligence.

In fact, although elements of truth could be found in all of these allegations, quite clearly most were exaggerated and out of proportion. There have been far too many instances of actual medical malpractice—some with very serious and some with less serious results. Scientific breakthroughs, enhanced physician training, access to and availability of medical care, all served to heighten both patient and professional expectations. Nonetheless, given the resources available, actual malpractice appeared the dominant explanation for the crisis.

In Washington State, a legislative package was introduced and passed in 1976 in an attempt to offer guidelines to meet the problem. It codified, for example, the ingredients of a proper informed consent; it clarified the concept of "standard of care." Collectively, the package was aimed at adding "reason and rationale" to what had become an adversarial relationship between patient and doctor. Many of its features were highly desirable even in the absence of any crisis.

At the same time, the Washington State Medical Association (WSMA) employed outside experts (Booze, Allen Consultants) to extract accurate data from the files of the state-sponsored insurance carrier (Aetna) and the Insurance Commissioner's Office, to confirm or refute once and forever the charge of mischievousness on the part of the insurance carrier. The resulting data did establish firmly that the cost of settlements and awards in Washington had been escalating at a compounding rate of some 22 percent per year for almost fifteen years. Premiums had to keep up. While in some years premiums were a bit too high, other years they were a bit too low; all in all, they were deemed to be reasonable. The carrier's premiums were vindicated.

This review, however, also revealed the philosophy of the insurance industry prevalent at the time. Since the industry had a built-in profit margin guaranteed as a percentage of premium income, it appeared to have no incentive to reduce premiums. Provided premiums were permitted to float, the industry's interests would hardly be served by efforts to curtail either allegations or settlements of malpractice. If successful, such efforts would only reduce premiums, which, in effect, would reduce derivative profit. This speculation seems to be supported by the lack of preventive action on the part of the insurance industry, although this was not necessarily a result of some nefarious scheme to bilk the public. Analyzing the data generated from the study would actually give one little, if any, confidence that a "data based" decision-making process was being used on the part of the insurance industry. From such evidence, one might easily conclude that the industry really did not know what was going on, or why, or what to do about it.

As similar reviews took place in other states, and as the concept of self-insurance took hold, changes in industry's attitude and practice have gradually emerged. One of the leading carriers, St. Paul, attempted to bring some order out of the chaos created by the "long tail" of the occurrence policy* by converting their entire line to claims-made formats. The resulting coverage protected the physician from any claims filed during a given calendar year, enhancing the predictability of the costs involved, in contrast to the occurrence policy which protected the physician from any suit, but which extended for the entire period of the policy. As a consequence, St. Paul had a far more precise technique by which to predict accurate premiums. Nevertheless, attempts nationwide by the industry to ameliorate the underlying malpractice problems have remained primitive at best.

The medical profession has initiated some forty "self-insurance companies" across the country since 1975 to better influence the total insurance process. Their aims are to involve individual physicians as active participants rather than simply passive observers, to reduce administrative costs, to improve underwriting measures (excluding poor risks), and to control claims management.

The review by Booze, Allen Consultants and its findings contributed to the formation in the state of Washington of a physician-sponsored self-insurance program in 1980. There, the aim was to exclude high-risk individuals and/or procedures, to return any surplus to the insureds (as opposed to stockholders), and, perhaps most importantly, to communicate to those insureds that any and all losses would be losses of their own money and not simply money from some inexhaustible reserve in Hartford, Connecticut.

In 1975 the Washington State legislature appropriated $90,000 to subject the Medical Disciplinary Board (housed within the Department of Licensing) to outside review; subsequently, the Board's mode of operation was drastically modified. Eventually, the Board mandated that hospital staffs, medical professional societies, third-party carriers, and malpractice carriers report specified sanctions imposed against physicians for the Board's review and possible disciplinary action. While the results have not been as beneficial as had initially been hoped (compliance with mandated reporting has fallen short

---

*A claim under an occurrence policy may be made "during the period of the policy or at any time in the future, subject only to the statute of limitations. . . . With this type of policy, the insurance company must charge enough to pay both current claims and any claims that occur during the long 'tail' of the policy" (Richards and Rathbun 1983:39).

of the goal), many efforts are underway to enhance their effectiveness (Goldsmith and Robertson 1980).

Other medical association activities were also implemented: pretrial hearing panels were set up; arbitration mechanisms and programs were established and evaluated; contact was made with the Insurance Commissioner's office, the Bar Association, and the State Supreme Court. All of these moves were attempts to bring relief of the malpractice crisis—with the improvements being viewed from the physician's perspective.

While these activities accelerated, the profession also began to address the basic question of whether there actually was any malpractice out there. One study commissioned by the Department of Health, Education and Welfare in the early 1970s found that 517 of 23,750 hospitalizations had documented evidence of "potentially compensable events" having occurred during the hospitalization—yet those led to only thirty malpractice actions.† The explanation from within the medical profession was that the "bad apples" consisted of 1 to 2 percent of physicians who were primarily untrained nonspecialists or unrealistic tertiary-care physicians in teaching centers. As subsequent data have been analyzed via reviews of closed claims, however, it has become obvious that while there was and is malpractice out there, its source is in no way limited to the suspected culprits. Even highly competent physicians seem unable to maintain their competency at all times, despite their apparent efforts to do so. *Malpractice involves the full spectrum of physician practitioners.*

One problem has arisen as the medical association and other organizations have looked into this issue. It is reminiscent of situations encountered by many of us as students in medical school and house officers in residency programs. We all participated in the design of very elaborate and complicated treatment plans for patients, while little was done to determine if the plans were ever put into effect, or if they worked. While many explanations are obvious, the fact is that follow-through was far less than ideal. It was as if the idea itself as opposed to its implementation was the ultimate goal. The result-

†Data from a report of the U.S. House of Representatives Committee on Interstate and Foreign Commerce: "An Overview of Medical Malpractice," 1975 (U.S. Government Printing Office, no. 48-5750).

ing attitude persists today. Elaborate treatment programs for the malpractice problem are mounted, usually without either opportunity for or serious commitment to follow-up or evaluation. Even the Physicians Insurance Association of America, dedicated to successful operations, did not begin to try to gather any group data about their success or failure until 1983. The result of failure to act is unwittingly to permit many causes of the malpractice problem to persist.

Today, in Washington, the medical association continues to provide information to the legislature, hoping to bring about tort reform. Because of a number of factors, including questions about the validity of the proposals and conflicting input from other segments of society, the 1983 tort reform program was not approved; that for 1984 proved equally ineffective. Moreover, many have concluded that a decade of attempted tort reform has been unsuccessful in altering the current malpractice situation and that another decade of effort is unlikely to fare better, at least in the eyes of physicians.

At the same time, physicians have begun to try to communicate more effectively among themselves, with their patients, and with allied health colleagues. Organized medicine has been pushing peer-review programs for physicians and introducing efforts to assist the "impaired physician" at all levels. In addition, efforts are underway to encourage medical staffs at hospitals to find out what actually is going on within the hospital.

In 1980, the Washington State Medical Association established a Risk Management Program designed to test actual compliance with predetermined standards of health care. The program consists of:

1. An ongoing, closed claims data-gathering program to serve as the basis for epidemiologic investigation about causes and/or associations.

2. An expanded Claims Review Panel to provide impartial physician review of malpractice claims to serve the interests of the defendant physician, his or her attorney, the involved carrier, and the profession as a whole.

3. A Professional Review Committee to assist underwriting by adjudicating insurability issues for new and renewal applicants, as well as "bad apples."

4. An Education Program aimed at helping members of the profession avoid allegations of malpractice and informing others about the ramifications of today's dilemma.

A cornerstone of the Risk Management Program is its Risk Management Review Units. To assist members in monitoring the effects of the educational effort (at least on the local scene), while preserving confidentiality, the WSMA Risk Management Program has developed and distributed a number of simple exercises which are, in essence, "ready to wear" audit programs for each hospital's quality assurance activity. Mandated by both the Joint Commission on Accreditation of Hospitals (JCAH) and the federally sponsored Washington Professional Standard Review Organization (WSPSRO), auditing of medical processes and outcomes against predetermined standards, with follow-up by designation, implementation, and evaluation of specific devices to overcome deficits, is the *modus operandi* of quality assurance programs.

The Risk Management Review Units provide guidance about where problems may exist and which solutions may be most effective. A description of this program and the review units themselves, as well as a listing of the topics involved, are contained in the Appendix. A preliminary survey of Washington's hospitals has determined that the units not only have been used, but have uncovered both suspected and unsuspected problems, and, more importantly, have stimulated appropriate corrective actions.

Sometimes simply documenting the degree of deficit in a practice will suffice to bring about change in an individual staff member's behavior; sometimes it will not. For example, when it surfaced that only 30 percent of physicians and .iurses washed their hands appropriately before entering "isolation rooms," discussions among the nursing staff involved did bring about a change in behavior. For these nurses, the percent complying with hand-washing regulations rose to and stayed at almost 90 percent (Robertson 1981).

A second element of the Risk Management Program has been the retrieval and publication in journal form of a series of case reports; many of these cases and an elaboration of the issues involved in each are presented in the following pages. For emphasis, most of the cases are taken from actual Washington experience; some have been slightly modified to retain anonymity. Designed to assume the format of conventional clinical case presentations, all of the cases and each of the topics have been selected to focus on issues thought to be remediable by changing physicians' individual or group behavior. Unfortunately, no quantifiable data are available to support or refute our claims of effectiveness. Certainly, some areas of controversy have diminished in intensity—e.g., convincing physicians that there is no alternative to seeking and documenting proper informed consent. Other areas of conflict seem to remain constant or evidence some growth in intensity—e.g., relationships with hospitals, as physicians and hospitals dispute responsibility for negligence actions.

The combination of justifiable concerns regarding confidentiality and less justifiable matters of individual and group self-interest make it most unlikely that quantifiable data will be available in the foreseeable future. Nonetheless, that is the eventual goal, so that the informed and involved physician can be confident that all of his or her colleagues are doing their best to ameliorate the malpractice crisis, and their patients and the public can be reassured that the profession is doing its utmost to discharge this professional obligation.

For ease of reference, I have categorized the cases and the topics involved so that, for example, one chapter and its several sections address the issue of physician-patient communication, while another focuses on the problem of peer review.‡ These Washington-based cases could just as easily have been taken from records of malpractice allegations in another state, and their applicability to physicians, hospitals, and health care administrators everywhere should be evident.

My aim in writing this book is to summarize where medicine stands in identifying malpractice-related problems and in implementing solutions, and to make available the Risk Management Review Units as a means for physicians, nurses, and hospitals to tackle the problem of malpractice (actual or perceived) head-on.

---

‡Additional contributions to the series are being prepared for subsequent inclusion in future issues of the *Western Journal of Medicine*, the official journal of the Washington State Medical Association, which has the fourth largest circulation in the country among medical journals.

2

Historical Setting

The term "malpractice" is derived from a 1697 English court decision. It was popularized by Sir William Blackstone in his "Commentaries"—a nineteenth-century British publication which brought many of the concepts of English law to America's lawyers. The first medical malpractice case to reach an appellate court in the United States did so in Connecticut in 1794; its resolution involved traditional common-law principles derived from our English heritage which, in the minds of some historians, are actually traceable to Grecian times.

In a recent review of medicological history in the United States, Frey (1982) attributes much of the origins of modern medico-legal thought to sixteenth-century Italy. Subsequently embellished by contributions from France and Germany, the basic ingredients of today's tort law saw little conceptual contribution from England. But because of our common language, the United States relied almost exclusively on English publications, such as Blackstone's, or English translations of German and French papers for its educational heritage.

Frey goes on to credit Benjamin Rush, the famous Philadelphia physician (1745?–1813), with the first American publication in the medico-legal field—a field which concentrated on forensic, toxicologic, and psychiatric issues in its early stages. Only in the 1860s after a significant rise in malpractice cases, did physician-lawyer John Elwell write the now famous *A Medico Legal Treatise on Malpractice and Medical Evidence Comprising the Element of Medical Jurisprudence.* Used extensively throughout the United States, Canada, and England, the book served to establish malpractice problems as an essential component of the medico-legal field. More than 90 percent of medical school graduates received medico-legal instruction in medical school by the turn of the century. Subsequently, there was a notable downturn in curricular attention corresponding with Flexner's scientific reformation of medical education aimed at returning it to the university setting. Practice-related matters were relegated to a secondary position. Only recently has there been an explosion of interest in and publications about malpractice, professional liability, and informed-consent issues, as a consequence of more specialization, technical advances, changes in social values, and the enormous increases in the costs of care, as well as increases in malpractice allegations per se.

In his review of the ancestry of malpractice law, Chapman (1982) emphasized that a critical ideologic change in the concept of physician responsibility had occurred in England during the fourteenth century. The change stemmed from the times of the bubonic plague and the 100 Years' War, and their decimation of population, and it had enormous implications for today's malpractice scene. Prior to the time of the landmark 1375 *Cavendish* decision, a physician was totally immune from any legal redress unless it could be shown that he or she had actually intended to do harm. Under *Cavendish*, however, a bad outcome due simply to the physician's negligence was deemed recoverable. This concept of professional negligence was first employed as the basis of a U.S. court's decision in 1853, with citation of the earlier English decision as its foundation. Chapman notes that "professional negligence is today usually defined as a standard of practice or professional action that is judged to be below what is usual and customary on the basis of expert testimony . . . (or) . . . that degree of skill and diligence employed by the ordinary practitioner in his field in the community or in similar communities at the time. The prudent practitioner is the analog of the common law's reasonable man."

This last point—the concept of a prudent physician and the reasonable man (patient)—has assumed increasing significance in the United States since Judge Benjamin N. Cardozo's decision of 1914 (*Schloendorff v. Society of New York Hospital*) emphasizing the inherent right of the individual to decide about submitting to surgery (Rosoff 1981). The Judge elaborated the legal principles underlying the right of the patient to be informed and to decide on his or her future— particularly before being subjected to a medical or surgical treatment. That decision serves as the foundation for the need of an informed consent today.

In many states, the test of the sufficiency of information given to the patient rests with the usual and customary "prudent physician practice"; in the state of Washington, however, the test rests with determining whether the information supplied would be sufficient to permit a reasonable patient to make an informed decision. Suffice it to note that in the 1980s any "prudent physician" will see to it that both tests are, in fact, satisfied. Legislation adopted in Washington in 1976 indicated that if the patient signed a statement that he or she had been informed, that signed statement served as *prima facie* evidence that an informed consent had been obtained. In its absence, the physician has to prove it was obtained; when it is present, however, the burden is on the patient to prove it had not been given.

As is predictable, each of the fifty states has numerous minor and some major differences in its respective legal statutes and case law determinations; it is their similarities which are so important. Washington's case law has contributed some landmark decisions that have drawn national attention (for example, *Miller v. Kennedy, Helling v. Carey, Smith v. Shannon, Harbeson v. Parke-Davis and USA*, and *In re: Bowman* 1980). In 1983, Washington's Supreme Court addressed the issue of "wrongful birth and wrongful life" and concluded that the physician has a responsibility, a duty, to provide available information to the pre-pregnant or pregnant patient that would permit her to decide whether to avoid or terminate a pregnancy. Failure to discharge that duty can be construed as negligence, and, if a baby is born impaired, damages are recoverable. As is obvious, the court's action has significant implications for the malpractice scene, further clarifying the extent of the physician's responsibilities and duties. But it also has significant social implications in emphasizing the right of the patient to seek abortion—in itself a continuing source of controversy.

Historically, the law in response to social change, like medicine in response to scientific advance, has evolved and continues to do so. Antiquated ideas are abandoned and social principles are adopted into the legal tenets. For example, more than seven hundred years have been consumed in reaching our current balance between the respective prerogatives of the king (government, the aristocracy, or the professional) and the rights of the citizen or common man. And that legal metamorphosis is likely to continue as the rights of the society (the group of "common men") emerge, sometimes to the advantage and sometimes to the detriment of the rights of the individual.

One other point worthy of emphasis is the legal profession's intense commitment to our current legal process—a process which maximizes the decision-making power of a judge or jury. The legal profession perceives it as essential and strives to maintain that mechanism of dispute resolution. Acknowledging the supremacy of this philosophy permits better understanding by nonlawyers of the reluctance of the lawyer to grant to anyone—and most particularly to the independent medical practitioner or to the medical profession—any statutory authority permitting either the individual or the group to make independent actions or decisions that would not be subject to review and reversal by a judge or a jury. Hence, physicians might do well to accept the fact that the standard of care as spelled out in any medical textbook or professional group's pronouncements will never be found 100 percent acceptable by the courts. Rather, as physicians we must realize that while we can mount a convincing case to establish a standard of care, periodically a judge or jury is likely to overrule that thesis. Understanding this proposition can help physicians comprehend why their own legal counsels so often seem to mumble when asked for seemingly simple "yes-no" answers. They, being lawyers, endorse the desirability of letting any finalities or certainties rest with the judge or jury.

When the medical malpractice crisis erupted in the early 1970s, surprisingly little authoritative data existed or were discoverable about where we stood as a nation: what were the costs, what were the losses, what were the problems. Individual communities and isolated carriers had some local data, but national data were conspicuous by their absence. Despite congressional investigations and studies carried out by several national commissions, a clear statistical picture was, and remains, difficult to draw. Obtaining the statistics is further impeded by the long tail of the occurrence policy, which remains the predominant medical malpractice insurance system within the United States. In actuality, the absence of such data tended to encourage much finger-pointing among virtually all participants on the medical malpractice scene—the physicians, the insurance companies, the patients, their attorneys, the courts.

As early as the 1940s, California had been identified as the bellwether for the country; its frequency of malpractice actions was noted to have risen faster than in any other state. It was California that enjoyed the notoriety of having the first million-dollar award; it ended up with at least three such awards prior to 1971. While today such awards might be considered commonplace and have occurred in more than half of the states, their rate of incline continues to rise. In the state of Washington, according to Booze, Allen Consultants, the rate of increase in *severity* (financial costs, including claims management, settlements, and awards) and in *frequency* of such occurrences led to substantial premium increases between 1963 and 1975. Subsequent data from Aetna to WSMA indicate that an exponential increment has continued.

Periodically, claims and counterclaims about solving the medical malpractice problem have surfaced; nonetheless, the rate of increase in costs continues to far outpace inflation. As of 1984, forty-one physician-sponsored insurance companies (and many enjoy the concomitant sponsorship of the state's organized medical society) have emerged to provide relief; they, too, continue to maintain healthy premiums to insure themselves against the possibility of going out of business. Significant differences do exist between premiums in different states, with California in the lead, while the midwestern and southeastern states bring up the rear. Although St. Paul's claims-made policies permit an actuarially far more predictable determination of premium, the majority of carriers continue to employ the occurrence policy, which may take as long as ten years or more to close out in terms of identifying final costs.

Complete, reliable data remain difficult to obtain, particularly as the competitive marketplace has resurfaced. Moreover, the issue of reinsurance costs, much of which are foreign-based, makes the determination of total costs even more difficult. When lack of data is combined with non-standard accounting procedures and the vagaries of investment income, precision of measurement seems an impossibility.

Thus the stage was set, in Washington State, for the intervention of the state medical association, stimulated by an ephemeral adversary which threatened the profession's image, its prestige, and its pocket book. In actuality, the medical association had first become enmeshed in the malpractice issue in the 1920s as it helped create a

"Medical Defense Fund," a quasi-insurance program committed to exonerating the physician. Whether a "conspiracy of silence" followed is not certain; what is certain is that the program subsequently experienced financial difficulties, insurance companies stepped in, their premiums climbed, until everyone recognized that the crisis was here.

The Risk Management Review Units presented in this volume were a logical, necessary, and beneficial outcome of the crisis, and they represent an innovative and practical approach to preventing medical malpractice.

3

Doctor-Patient Communication

Felt by many to be pivotal to the malpractice crisis, difficulties in doctor-patient communication are more prevalent and permeating than has been imagined. A top target for doctors' attention, the subject demands far more objective study and concentrated training than it has received in the past (Robertson 1983). It is apparent that the opportunity for misunderstanding or for faulty communication is increasing with telephone technology and the resulting lack of face-to-face interaction, but many other factors are also contributory. Specialization forces the already anxious patient to deal with two, three, or more strangers. Hospitalization compounds the problem of different faces, different emphasis, different advice. Patients' expectations have changed dramatically in the last few decades. As short a time ago as 1915, the average patient entering a hospital had at least a 50:50 chance of not leaving it alive. Few today can easily accept that possibility. In addition, costs (plus worries about costs) are up.

More than ever, the medical profession must improve its individual and collective performances in dealing with patients and their problems. The following case studies highlight some examples of communication failures.

Section 1.   Communication Breakdown
Section 2.   Communication Failures in the Hospital
Section 3.   Communication Problems in the Office

17

SECTION 1

Communication Breakdown

Case 1. P. A., a 2,245-gram premature infant, was suspected at 36 hours of age of being septic. Following a thorough physical examination, a chest film, and appropriate cultures, antibiotic therapy was begun with ampicillin and Gentamicin. Somehow in transmitting the drug order to the pharmacy, a decimal-place error was made; as a result the infant received a 10-fold overdose of Gentamicin for two successive doses. Fortunately, the pharmacy's routine quality control program then detected the discrepancy and promptly sought consultation regarding potential management options from the regional poison center and the manufacturer. Based on the then best available information, no further treatment other than continual hydration was recommended, and the patient appeared to be doing well. More than a year later his ambulation, hearing, and renal functions were all evaluated as normal. Nonetheless, it is obvious that the communication error would have resulted in a significant medical problem had it not been detected and corrected so promptly.

Case 2. K. N., a 44-year-old married female, had been admitted to the hospital with a mild depression. Over the next two weeks some details of her life came to light, and her situational depression appeared to respond well to supportive psychotherapy and antidepressant medication. Following her discharge on a Sunday, her physician promptly dictated a summary letter, including several of the situational details. Midway through the dictation, the recording device—on a trial basis at the hospital—ceased to function. The next morning, the company representative picked up the machine including the tape. After making necessary repairs, he checked out the machine by listening to the tape. He then took the machine plus the tape to his supervisor who, unbelievably, was the husband of the patient involved! Needless to say, the husband was incensed and made threats of violence as well as legal action. While he was eventually dissuaded by the distraught attending psychiatrist, the communication problem is self evident; confidentiality was breached.

Case 3. E. D., a 29-year-old unmarried female, had a long history of recurrent lower abdominal pain. On several occasions she had been examined by her physician who had made a repeated diagnosis of chronic pelvic inflammatory disease. Each time she was treated accordingly, but with only temporary improvement.

One Tuesday morning, she called her physician's office seeking an appointment because her symptoms were recurring. Answered in what she sensed was a hostile fashion by a staff member—who later admitted to being impatient with her prior behavior and "general attitude—the patient accepted a reappointment 11 days later. That evening, the physician, to his consternation, was contacted by the emergency room because his patient had arrived there with a ruptured ectopic pregnancy. While the outcome of the case was entirely as expected and thus no damages were identified, the physician endured many months of anxiety over threatened lawsuits because of the attitude and actions of the office staff member.

Discussion

Each of these cases demonstrates one or more disasters in communication. As is obvious, the opportunities for such disasters occur many times daily. Every time a physician talks with a patient, a staff member answers the telephone, or a hospital staff nurse carries out an order, the chance for communication failure looms large. Moreover, the likelihood of such failure increases when the patient is anxious or upset just as it does when the physician or the staff is overcommitted and overworked. In those situations, the involved parties themselves prove to be, in effect, faulty originators or faulty receivers of a message.

Sometimes it is the message, or the words we use to convey that message, that is at fault. Consider the following examples. Lists of more than a thousand sound-alike and look-alike drug names have been compiled (see B. Teplitsky, *Pharmacy Times,* November 1979)—Ananase versus Orinase, Chonidine versus Quinidine, Donnatal versus Dianabol, Mellaril versus Moderil, Serax versus Xerac, Tegretol versus Demerol—the list goes on. The resulting confusion can be avoided only by rigorous adherence to written rather than verbal orders and through careful and clear handwriting.

Data from Children's Orthopedic Hospital in Seattle (Tso and Robertson 1980) attest to the fact that legibility of prescriptions in hospitals leaves far too much to be desired. Pharmacists spend an inordinate amount of time attempting to validate or verify uninterpretable messages at the cost of much time, effort, and dollars—assuming that they are able to be certain which prescriptions qualify for such careful followup. In a subsequent study at Children's, some 30 percent of physicians' signatures on consultation notes were judged indecipherable by three independent evaluators. One could shrug and mumble, "That can never be changed," and continue to pay larger insurance premiums to cover the resulting errors. Or one can seize the initiative to correct the problem, for example, requiring offending staff members to carry and use stamps with their printed name plus signature, which are then initialed by the physician for verification.

Each JCAH-accredited hospital is required to have a list of approved abbreviations for use therein. Again at Children's Orthopedic Hospital, such a list was dutifully prepared and filed. The only problem was that when 26 randomly selected abbreviations from the list were posed to members of the staff, only one person among 58 respondents could interpret more than half of the sample. Does DPT, for example, mean demerol, phenergan, and thorazine or diphtheria, pertussis, and tetanus? Obviously, were the abbreviations used in context, recognition rates would probably be higher, but the likelihood of communication errors remains high. Conclusion: avoid abbreviations in medical records.

Every one of us uses the telephone. However, its use limits the self-correction we can make when we watch a colleague's or a patient's facial expressions. Keep that in mind when using the phone. Clarify instructions as best you can and permit your listeners to ask questions. Try not to hurry them, and keep documentation of all telephone calls for your office records.

The account executive of a large insurance carrier recently commented, "If only more physicians realized that how they and their staffs come across to patients determines in a large part how individual patients will react to less than ideal treatment. Similarly if physicians only realized that how they come across to their staffs or to their hospital colleagues is equally critical in determining how those people represent them to their patients. At all times that representation ought to be the best possible."

What You Can Do

In your office, do you periodically review communication procedures and practices with your staff and your colleagues to try to minimize problems? Have you implemented a recording program for telephone messages?

In your practice, do you exert extra care when dealing with drugs which have similar sounding names or which appear comparable in print? Do you avoid verbal orders? In your hospital, are you strongly supportive of efforts to eliminate verbal orders?

In your office records or your hospital notes, are you doing your best to enhance legibility and avoid ambiguous abbreviations?

Fifty years ago the medical record was largely a notebook of reminders for the doctor's use. Today that record is a communication vehicle for scores of professionals and staff. It ought to prevent problems rather than create them. Do your part in making medical records serve you and your patients.

SECTION 2

Communication Failures in the Hospital

Case 1.   R. P. and T. P., a set of premature twins, weighed 1,380 grams and 1,430 grams, respectively, at birth. Completing an uneventful postnatal period, they gained weight appropriately and were ready for discharge home at approximately eight weeks. T. P.'s discharge preceded R. P.'s by some ten days in order to assure that the primiparous mother (who had, however, already reared several foster and adopted children) was prepared for each arrival.

Plans for their feeding included continuing the prepared formula used in the hospital, which was constructed from a powdered preparation, with one measure of powder being diluted in two ounces of water. This information allegedly was verbally transmitted to the mother prior to discharge of the first twin. Some ten days later, comparable instructions accompanied the discharge of the second twin— but again no written instructions were provided. Subsequently, the mother consulted her local physician, who, upon hearing the formula details, urged the mother to change the ratio of components to 1:1. When the mother returned to the hospital for a routine follow-up of the infants' progress, the 1:2 proportion ratio was stressed again (verbally) and apparently this time she misconstrued it as 2:1.

To abbreviate the case details, both infants contracted diarrhea with rapid signs of dehydration. The twins were brought back to the local physician, who recognized that both infants were severely ill and arranged for immediate hospitalization. Unfortunately, T. P. succumbed in transit. R. P. arrived with serum sodium of 196 mEq per liter, directly attributable to the overly concentrated formula. Later he was diagnosed as having associated neurological problems.

Due to the near-total breakdown in communication, both formal and informal, between all parties involved, a successful suit resulted in a sizeable award against the physicians, the hospital, and the manufacturer.

Case 2. J. M., a 21-year-old male, was admitted to the hospital via the emergency room on a Friday night following a motorcycle accident in which he sustained multiple lacerations, numerous contusions, and a fracture of his femur and radius. Among other steps taken, orders were written for "neuro checks every two hours." On Saturday morning, J. M., was noted to have become progressively obtunded with a rising blood pressure and a slowing heart rate, but the attending physician was not notified, allegedly because of some misinterpretation of the orders. While J. M.'s subdural hematoma was successfully localized by CT scan and evacuated without complication, considerable and heated discussion occurred among the professional staff about the cause of the delayed diagnosis and the concurrent risk to the patient. When cooler heads eventually prevailed, the staff agreed to seek a more consistent understanding of the variety of orders written in the order book, which had to be interpreted by many different individuals.

Case 3. W. D., a 19-year-old male, suffered an apparent fractured tibia during football practice. He was taken to a hospital emergency room where he was x-rayed and the diagnosis established. He was then admitted to the hospital; initial management included sedation, traction, and casting. During the night he complained of increasing discomfort and pain in his foot. By morning rounds, discoloration was apparent and heroic measures were employed in an effort to avoid amputation, with eventual success but with notable loss of function.

While initial discussions concluded that the nursing staff had failed to recognize any problem, a more detailed investigation revealed that the nurse had, in fact, recognized that a problem existed but had interpreted it as being a relatively minor one. She had been reluctant to call the attending physician because of his widespread reputation for being inconsiderate, overbearing, opinionated, disrespectful, and a "bear" when disturbed at night. That reputation had accompanied him to the hospital and stayed with him during his time there. After the malpractice suit was settled in favor of the plaintiff, the question about what should be done to alter the physician's behavior in the future was aired.

Discussion

The focus of these case reports is directed toward communication problems between physicians and their patients, as well as among physicians themselves and in their interactions with their nursing colleagues. The cases provide examples of how words, phrases, and attitudes can, in themselves, contribute to a breakdown in the communication process.

The past several years have seen programs instituted to alleviate the communication difficulties between physicians and patients, as well as among health professionals. Efforts are underway nationally to address the problems and introduce some solutions, e.g., increasing the readability of informed consent forms and encouraging more open communication between nurses and physicians. One such effort originated in Canada.

In 1980, two Canadian physicians, Bryant and Norman, concerned about physician-to-physician communication, selected 30 terms used frequently in hospital reports—such as "probably," "sometimes," and "unlikely"—which seemed subject to repeated misinterpretations or differences in interpretation by different physicians. They asked a group of hospital-based Canadian physicians to specify on a scale of 0 to 100 percent the likelihood of a disease being present as indicated by each term. The results showed a wide range in meaning as perceived by the respondents. For example, the likelihood of a disease being present as indicated by the term "sometimes" extended from a low of 5 percent of the time to a high of 75 percent of the time. Most of the ranges exceeded 50 percent.

When this exercise was replicated in Seattle, physicians not only paralleled remarkably closely the means derived from the Canadian group, but also paralleled the wide variation in specific interpretations by individual respondents. Finding the results so similar, we are left with the question, "Do patients also 'misinterpret' these terms? If so, can such terms be used to communicate effectively with patients when doctors are seeking and securing an informed consent?"

Some indication of the answer was found from repeating the study—first among 80 graduate students in the University of Washington School of Business Administration and then among the Board of Trustees at the Children's Orthopedic Hospital and Medical Center in Seattle. Table 1 confirms the remarkable similarity of the means or average interpretations derived from each of the four groups; note how the degree of likelihood is virtually constant from group to group. But in Table 2, also note the wide ranges of interpretation reported among the individuals within each group, making any semblance of consistency in individual interpretation virtually impossible.

Some might naturally conclude that in discussing with a patient the likelihood of a complication from drug treatment or surgery, one would do well to avoid the use of ambiguous terms and resort instead to expressing likelihoods in percentiles, much as do our weather broadcasters—e.g., "you have a 10 percent chance of a postoperative complication" (see Robertson 1983).

TABLE 1. Quantifying Word Meanings

Term	NEJM 1980	Seattle M.D.s	UW MBAs	COHMC B/T
Always	99 ± 2*	98 ± 6	98 ± 3	100 ± 0
Often	61 ± 13	59 ± 17	61 ± 16	57 ± 13
Sometimes	33 ± 17	34 ± 16	38 ± 12	37 ± 21
On Occasion	12 ± 7	20 ± 16	20 ± 10	18 ± 21
Rarely	5 ± 4	15 ± 34	12 ± 20	23 ± 36

*Mean ± S.D. shown in percentages

TABLE 2. Quantifying Word Meanings

Term	NEJM 1980	Seattle M.D.s	UW MBAs	COHMC B/T
Always	90–100*	60–100	80–100	100–
Often	30– 80	20– 90	20– 90	20–90
Sometimes	10– 60	0– 90	10– 60	10–70
On Occasion	0– 20	0– 70	5– 50	10–60
Rarely	0– 10	0– 95	0– 90	0–60

*Range shown in percentages

In addition to the choice of words used to communicate, the atmosphere in which they are exchanged remains important. As noted in cases 2 and 3, had mutually reinforcing attitudes been present on behalf of the professionals involved, both problems probably would have been avoided. Some experts hold that the most significant contributors to allegations of malpractice are the "passing shots," the innuendoes, the outright counterstatements made to patients by the attending physician's colleagues.

What You Can Do

In your hospital, is there a physician-nurse liaison committee to address interprofessional communication problems, particularly those relating to writing orders, observing patients, and handling patient complaints?

In your community, assuming you have two or more hospitals, what has been done to standardize routines so that inadvertent oversights can be avoided when markedly dissimilar routines are employed in different hospitals? What—if anything—are your county's physicians doing to ameliorate such problems?

Risk management programs across the country are recognizing that improvement in communication is most likely to foster fewer allegations of malpractice and that physicians can enhance doctor-patient and interprofessional communication. Don't let crossed-wires drag you into a malpractice suit.

SECTION 3

Communication Problems in the Office

Case 1. D. W., a 34-year-old female, visited her gynecologist, Dr. L. M., for a routine exam, including Pap smear. Upon completing the exam, Dr. M. told D. W. that he would call her if the report from the Pap smear were abnormal. The lab report, received on the Friday of an extended weekend, *was* abnormal, and Dr. M. wrote a note to his assistant to call D. W. and arrange for an appointment the next week.

After one or two unsuccessful attempts to reach D. W. by telephone, Dr. M.'s assistant set the note aside, intending to try again later. However, the note somehow got lost, and the assistant forgot about the matter. Dr. M. assumed that the appointment had been made, but failed to notice that D. W. did not return. In fact, he also forgot. About a year later, D. W. was diagnosed by another doctor as having cervical cancer which had metastasized. She died several months later. Her family received a $750,000 award.

Case 2. A. B., a three-year-old female, had been spiking high temperatures for about a day and a half. Unable to "break" her fever, her mother called her physician's office to make an appointment. Upon learning that the doctor was out of town for several days, A. B.'s mother asked the receptionist if she had any suggestions. The receptionist told the mother that the symptoms sounded like the flu that was going around and suggested she give the child aspirin and fluids and call back in a few days if the child didn't get better.

After two days of persistent high fever, the mother took A. B. to the local emergency room, where the child was diagnosed as having meningitis. Although heroic efforts were employed, A. B. died the following day. Her parents filed a malpractice suit against the doctor and his receptionist. The case was settled out of court for $500,000.

Case 3. K. J., a 54-year-old large and overweight woman, had been seeing Dr. L. A., her family physician, for some time complaining about vague abdominal pains. Yet whenever Dr. A. scheduled her for tests or follow-up appointments, she repeatedly canceled or failed to appear.

One night when her abdominal pain became particularly severe, she went to a hospital emergency room and subsequently underwent surgical exploration for what proved to be a ruptured gall bladder, which led to extended hospitalization. K. J. subsequently brought suit against Dr. A., alleging that he had failed to diagnose her condition.

Fortunately, Dr. A.'s assistant had meticulously recorded every cancellation, no show, and other evidence of non-cooperation. Upon seeing these well-documented office records, K. J.'s attorney quickly dropped the suit.

Discussion

Currently, most malpractice cases have their origins in the hospital; nonetheless, a significant minority (approximately 20–30 percent) stem from what goes on or fails to go on in the physician's office. As the basis of malpractice actions is clearly shifting away from surgical mishaps to encompass diagnostic failures and drug-related problems, office-based cases will assume even more importance. Moreover, considerable evidence suggests that what transpires in the office, what kinds of relationships are developed there, may actually be paramount in setting the stage for a patient's subsequent reaction if there are problems in treatment. In November 1981, *American Medical News* highlighted R. M. Anderson's patient survey about patient's perceptions of office settings. Consider a few items that may have a familiar ring.

Being kept waiting proved particularly objectionable. Most patients seemed prepared to accept 15 minutes as no problem; 85 percent were prepared to accept up to half an hour's delay. But virtually none could tolerate tardiness of an hour or more in keeping an appointment. Anderson also found that the time spent with the physician correlated well with satisfied patients. Again, virtually none who spent 25 minutes or more with the physician had any sense of frustration or dissatisfaction whatsoever. Many who spent significantly less time were also entirely satisfied, provided the specific problem at hand lent itself to speedy resolution. But a sizeable number found brief visits inadequate for their problem, leading to appointment breaking, changing physicians, or just plain hostility. Such data have practical import when viewed against a 1981 Robert Wood Johnson survey of office practice performance in which internists, pediatricians, and family physicians all averaged no more than 15 minutes for their office visits. The wise physician and his or her office staff will be on the lookout for those patients whose needs require extended contact time, and will act accordingly. The length of the visits often correlated with the patient's perception of how much information the physician actually provided; the more information given, the more satisfied the patient. Whether, in fact, the patients were addressing information per se or the opportunity of discussion remains obscure, but "time for talk" was critical.

Since the 1975 Washington legislature adopted WSMA's proposal to clarify the ingredients of informed consents, disputes over their adequacy appear to have been drastically curtailed. Since 1975, when the issues began to be discussed and documented on WSMA-sponsored forms, "lack of informed consent" has not served as a basic factor for any malpractice actions. Many experts suggest that securing informed consent in the office before the patient comes to the hustle and bustle of the hospital's preoperative setting reduces the likelihood of negligence action. Some add, appropriately, that the same type of discussion and documentation given to surgical issues which take place in the office is also needed when unusual or new drugs are being employed. Caution is the watchword; the patient's involvement in the decision must be appropriately documented.

Documentation is as critical in the office as it is in the hospital. Two areas of trouble appear to be cropping up more and more frequently. The first has to do with telephone calls and patient management. Any office-based practitioner knows how much the phone contact means; while documenting every call is a nuisance and creates additional effort, paperwork, and cost, more and more doctors are making sure the job gets done. At the Seattle Poison Center, for example, we document on a simple written record important points of more than 60,000 phone calls per year. The job can be done, but there has to be a commitment to it. Admittedly, there is an associated cost, but the cost can well be a lot less than a malpractice action.

The second major problem in the office, as well as in the hospital, continues to wreak havoc: *the altered record*. No successful defense is possible with an altered record (a point made in the movie *The Verdict*). Remember: records can be modified—material can be added or deleted—so long as the process is up front and identified. However, when additions are made or "corrections" inserted in such a fashion as to try to impress the reader that they were part of the original note, that's when a problem arises. For some reason, a few physicians and their office staffs persist in such falsification. The Oregon Medical Association's anti-malpractice program stresses avoiding altering records, and yet at least four physicians have altered a medical record within six months of having participated in their program.

What You Can Do

In your office, have you considered sitting down with your staff to review your collective successes or shortcomings in dealing with patients—appointment schedules, waiting times, promptness in billing, telephone courtesy, and other efforts to create a pleasant relationship? If you have, have you really listened to the staff's ideas? Are your decisions then put into action?

How do you actually know what patients think of your program? Many hospitals and large clinics employ simple "opinionnaires" for patients to complete regarding their experience during a visit; have you considered using one? The American Medical Association makes such a questionnaire available to measure patient satisfaction.*

In your office, have you introduced a policy and program to document phone calls? Have you taken a leadership position, serving as a role model to get the job done? Do you also document calls at night and on weekends? Finally, can you be certain you and your staff will not be susceptible to charges of altering records, i.e., introducing changes in what could be construed as a deceptive manner? Have you ever reviewed your charts with this in mind? As cost-containment efforts encourage all of us to do more in our offices as opposed to our hospitals, the opportunity for error may increase. Now is the time to introduce a "prophylactic program" to avoid such consequences.

---

*"The Patient Survey Questionnaire," OP-121, available from AMA, P.O. Box 10946, Chicago, Illinois 60610, $8.00 per 100 prepaid plus $1.50 handling charge.

4

Informed Consent

Still an evolving philosophic concept, the extent of the rights of an individual patient to determine his or her future is a critical issue of debate. At the turn of the century, few, if any, challenged the authority of the physician, much less the surgeon. During World War II, far too many GIs had their tonsils out, their hemorrhoids tied, or their foreskins circumcised at the whim of the battalion surgeon. Who was to say "no"? That heritage is passé; today the patient is involved in the decision-making as never before. Sometimes so much attention is devoted to obtaining appropriate consents that the ideal times for medical or surgical intervention pass by. But most think the risk worth the benefits. As a consequence, one point is clear: the physician is in no way the sole decision maker. The "reasonable" patient is king and the "prudent" physician will act accordingly.

SECTION 4

Failure to Inform of Material Risks

Case 1. A. B., a 46-year-old blue-collar worker, had been seeing an orthopedist intermittently for episodic back and knee pain. Despite conservative therapy, symptoms progressed. Myelogram revealed a "complete L3–L4 block" and subsequent exploration uncovered a herniated disc, a large component of which was removed without prior discussion of potential complication with the patient. Immediately upon awakening, A. B. reported bilateral lower leg weakness and diminished sensation. Subsequently a diagnosis of "cauda equina syndrome" was made, probably due to excessive intra-operative traction, which in turn led to total occupational disability and the filing of a malpractice suit.

The case was heard by a Claims Review Panel which recommended that it be settled. The insurance company agreed to a sum of more than $200,000. While many factors contributed to the panel's recommendation (contrasting professional opinions about the standard of care involved, the operative experience of the surgeon, conflicting hospital and office notes, as well as the operative findings at re-exploration), one particular issue stood out: lack of informed consent.

The patient denied he was ever informed of any possible risks of the procedure or alternatives to it. The hospital and office records were both devoid of any evidence of the patient's having consented to the procedure, and the doctor admitted that it had not been his practice to document such details or to obtain a signed informed consent from patients undergoing such procedures.

Case 2. E. M., a 34-year-old grossly obese male, underwent an intestinal by-pass procedure to lose weight. The surgical event itself was complicated only by a mild suture line infection, which responded quickly to treatment. The postoperative year, however, was a disaster in the patient's eyes, in that he had debilitating diarrhea and was totally unable to work. He filed a malpractice suit alleging not only faulty surgical techniques, but also failure to inform him of the possible negative consequences. Unfortunately, no record documenting an informed consent discussion was found; prompt settlement followed.

Case 3. M. S., a 38-year-old woman, had been using birth control pills for almost six years; without warning she had a stroke resulting in partial permanent neurologic disability. She brought a negligence action against the prescribing physician, alleging that she had never been informed by him of the potential risks involved. No record of consent was found. She was successful in achieving a sizeable award.

Discussion

In reviewing both old and new Washington malpractice claims, informed consent crops up again and again as an issue. Many times it serves simply to indicate that poor communication took place between doctor and patient; in other instances it appears that the patient in retrospect felt unduly pressured. Occasionally, it seems to be raised simply as a legal gimmick. Nonetheless, much misunderstanding persists among physicians and other health professionals about the concepts involved. To clarify them, Leslie J. Miller, a member of the AMA Division of Corporate Law, presented a four-part series in the *Journal of the American Medical Association* (November 21 and 28 and December 5 and 12, 1980). A few points warrant emphasis:

By Washington statute, physicians are obliged to adopt the "material risk to a reasonable person" approach to informed consent. This is in contrast to the "community's professional standards" approach. The former focuses on the patient's perception; the latter, on the professional standard. In Washington, the adequacy of the informed consent process is to be measured by the test: "Was adequate information provided so that a reasonable person could make an informed choice?" In addition, the wise physician will continue to ask himself or herself: "Am I also abiding by what I perceive as our community professional standards?" Many attorneys feel that both elements ought to be addressed.

Under Washington statute, if the competent patient signs an appropriate form or statement acknowledging that he or she has been informed about the contemplated procedure, its probable outcome, its material risks, the alternatives available and their risks, as well as the option of no treatment and its risks, such a document serves as *prima facie* evidence that an adequate informed consent has been given. In legal terms this means that should the patient or his or her counsel seek to claim inadequate informed consent, they will have to prove that the physician failed to satisfy the test mentioned above. In the absence of an appropriately completed form, however, it is up to the physician to prove that he or she did inform the patient adequately. It is to the physician's advantage to force the plaintiff to do the proving by securing an adequately documented consent.

While "risk" is purposely not precisely defined in the statutes, whether or not a risk is "material" is a function of the likelihood of its occurrence, the severity of the injury it threatens to cause, as well as the existence of reasonable alternatives. As Miller stresses, a material risk is one that "a reasonable person"—in what the physician knows or should know to be that patient's position—would be likely to consider significant in deciding whether or not to undertake the proposed therapy.

In the climate of the 1980s, a physician would be unwise to invoke the "therapeutic privilege" defense in not seeking an informed consent, that is, claiming that a complete and candid disclosure was not possible because of the possible effects on the physical or emotional well-being of the patient. Such an argument is loaded with uncertainty. If it is ever to be invoked, a carefully documented second, third, or possibly fourth opinion or consultation ought to be obtained.

Miller concludes with five recommendations:
1. The doctor should personally talk with the patient.
2. The information conveyed should be in intelligible form.
3. Promises of "no risk" should be avoided.
4. If an emergency exists so that the patient is unable to consent, a spouse or relative should be informed; this will help establish the doctor's concern about the patient's welfare.
5. All discussions and procedures should be documented.

In Washington, disputes about informed consent play a role—though not necessarily a primary role—in at least 25 percent of the malpractice cases. To the best of my knowledge, there has been no successful claim involving a WSMA-approved informed consent form. Consequently, the WSMA urges that their form or an analogous one be adopted and used in every hospital across the state. Unfortunately, more than five years after the informed consent statute was passed, some hospitals and their medical staffs have yet to adopt this practice; in truth, they are playing Russian roulette, and with your permission!

What You Can Do

Do you always inform your patients when significant risks are involved? Do you always document discussions in the record and obtain the patient's (or his or her representative's) written consent? Do your partners or associates always follow such a course of action? Does your hospital's medical staff always follow such a course of action?

In your hospital, is the WSMA form or an analogous form completed and clearly retrievable in the chart? Who is responsible for monitoring adequate completion of such forms? Is a periodic report of compliance provided to the medical staff? Just what happens to the non-complying physician?

Appropriate involvement of the patient is beneficial to all involved—the patient, the family, the physician, the hospital, and the insurance carrier.

SECTION 5

Failure to Obtain Consent

Case 1. T. S., a five-year-old male, had repeated bouts of pharyngitis and otitis media; both the parents and the physician became impatient with the frequent recurrences and apparent failure of both therapeutic and prophylactic antibiotics. T. S. was referred to an otolaryngologist who diagnosed extensive adenoiditis and recommended adenoidectomy. All went well during the hospitalization, induction of anesthesia, and procedure. However, as the procedure was being terminated, the surgeon decided to remove a segment of one hypertrophied tonsil. Just as he did so, the boy suffered a cardiac arrest, with permanent severe neurological damage.

A major contribution to the staggering amount of the subsequent settlement was the most obvious lack of informed consent for the removal of the tonsil. The issue of tonsillectomy apparently simply hadn't come up. The surgeon assumed that were he to proceed, it would eliminate the risk of another anesthesia; but the parents weren't in on the decision.

Case 2. S. P., a 37-year-old mother of three, decided she would seek tubal ligation as her contraceptive technique. For several years, she had been bothered by ulcer symptoms, and, following an extensive work-up including radioimmune assays for gastrin, had been diagnosed as having Zollinger-Ellison Syndrome. Its causes and consequences had been extensively discussed with her, but she had remained adamant that surgery was out of the question for her.

When the tubal ligation was performed under general anesthesia via laparotomy, the operating gynecologist inspected the abdominal contents and detected a pancreatic mass. He called in a general surgeon who confirmed the finding and arranged to biopsy the mass. Postoperatively, the patient developed complications and pancreatitis, and, subsequently, alleged that there had been no informed consent in the case. A successful lawsuit followed.

Case 3. S. C., a 27-year-old-woman, delivered her firstborn son in the hospital without any unusual occurrences; he weighed 8 pounds 2 ounces. His hospital course was equally uneventful—save for the occurrence of an unrequested circumcision. Retrospectively, it was determined that his mother had been approached by a hospital staff member with the familiar questions of whether to feed by breast or bottle, and whether or not to circumcise. While the mother's answer was documented in the chart, somehow a slip-up occurred and the child was circumcised on the morning of discharge, without any additional discussion with the mother. The mother and father alleged both a lack of informed consent and a disregard for their wishes. In this instance, a claim was filed but eventually dropped.

Discussion

Common sense says that these three cases must be either figments of the imagination or at least 60 years old. The reality, however, is that they are real and that they are all too current. Each case points to the basic issue of informed consent—society's assurance of the patient's right to determine his or her body's destiny.

In some medical circles, it seems popular to argue that the informed consent issue is really a smokescreen, or an imaginary ogre primarily responsible for the program of many medical gatherings, but not a significant factor in the malpractice field. Others stress, I think more correctly, that informed consent remains a critical issue; that it ought to be serving as a warning light to the profession of society's intention to redress the "balance of power" between physicians and the public.

While distinctions exist among states on the specifics of an appropriate informed consent, the basic purpose of such statutes is absolutely clear: the patient is, at the very least, a partner in the decision-making process. This reflects a change in society's thinking, and, one hopes, in physicians' practices. For example, many readers will recall medical school days of yesteryear when large groups of students learned to do pelvic examination on anesthetized patients who were oblivious of what was going on. Today, a patient's prerogatives have been established and recognized, and such a practice would not be tolerated. The students have benefited, too, as they can learn much more adequately the techniques involved from an alert, cooperative patient.

Lest one conclude that informed consent is an overplayed theme, I visited a Washington hospital early in 1982 and listened to a debate on whether or not the medical staff rules and regulations ought to require physicians both to secure and to document informed consents in the chart. In 1982, the issue was still under debate! Looked at differently, some physicians were still debating whether or not to join the rest of the profession in accepting society's demands, on the one hand to assure patients of their rights, and on the other to minimize malpractice actions. Some of these same physicians had attacked attorneys and pleaded with the legislature to correct the malpractice problem which they themselves perpetuated. Can we as a profession permit such practices to continue? Isn't the risk to all concerned too great? Isn't it time to call a halt to nonparticipation?

What You Can Do

In your hospital, is there an ongoing review of the adequacy of both obtaining and documenting informed consents? Who precisely is responsible? Is the medical staff informed of the review findings? Has anyone ever verified, or considered verifying, the accuracy of the documentation available?

What (if any) sanctions are imposed on a physician who is remiss in his or her responsibility? Have such sanctions ever been imposed? How would an appeal from them be handled?

While legal disputes will no doubt continue regarding the adequacy of informed consent, many disputes could be totally avoided if the entire profession complied with current expectations and statutes. The costs of not doing so are simply prohibitive.

SECTION 6

The Rights of the State; the Limits of Consent

Case 1. J. J., a 31-year-old-multiparous housewife, had sought routine prenatal care at a Georgia hospital. As she neared term, the examining physician detected placenta previa and gave an opinion that were vaginal delivery attempted there would be a 99 percent chance that the child would die and a 50 percent chance that the mother would also die. Consequently, he strongly recommended Cesarean section. J. J., the wife of a fundamentalist minister, refused to consent to an operation, objecting on religious grounds. She steadfastly held that "God would heal her."

In her thirty-ninth week of gestation, the hospital petitioned the Superior Court for an order authorizing its agent to perform a Cesarean section, a sonogram, and any necessary blood transfusions. Such authorization was granted. The next day the county's Department of Family and Children's Services (acting on behalf of the state's Department of Human Resources) secured a conclusion from the court that the fetus was a "deprived child." It was granted custody of the fetus and the sheriff was authorized to transport the patient to the hospital for a section. J. J. and her husband appealed to the Georgia Supreme Court, which, after due consideration, affirmed the lower court's judgment, thus establishing a controversial legal precedent and a cause of considerable speculation. Interestingly, J. J. later arrived at the hospital voluntarily and precipitated an apparently normal vaginal delivery of a normal child—but not until after the judicial rulings. Both mother and child did well.

Discussion

The issues here are both simple and complex—since the rights of the two parties are in obvious conflict and the obligations and prerogatives of the state and its physicians are a bit fuzzy. The court's actions were apparently predicated on relative balance between the state's interest in protecting the unborn child, and the mother's rights of privacy and religious freedom. (Consider the similarity of the is-

sues to those under debate with "Baby Doe" in New York.) Others
have concluded that the Georgia court's decision was an infringement on at least three distinct rights of the mother: her right to religious freedom, her right of refusal to medical treatment, and her
right of parental autonomy in matters affecting the family.

The court, in denying those rights and authorizing the state's intrusion, relied on *Roe v. Wade,* the U.S. Supreme Court decision of
the early 1970s that set the stage for the nation's current legal position on abortion and the timing of "viability." It established a policy
that the state may prohibit abortion, but only after "viability" has
been reached. In this instance the court concluded that, since viability had been reached, it had the responsibility to intrude. But note
the conceptual leap made by the Georgia court. One case involved
outlawing a surgical procedure (abortion), while the other compelled
a surgical procedure (Cesarean section). Although the court cited
specific case law precedents to support its override of the right to
religious freedom and the right to refuse medical treatment, it cited
no specific case law to override the issue of family autonomy. Instead, it relied on commonly accepted ideas of the "state's compelling
interest" in any child, allowing judicially compelled blood transfusions, surgical procedures, and mandatory custody outside the home.

In light of the "Baby Doe conflict" this case has particular perti-
nence. In "Baby Doe," both the lower court and the appellate court
have ruled in favor of parental privacy as opposed to the state's compelling interest to protect the child under 504. Will that position be
sustained at the U.S. Supreme Court level?

Using the Georgia court's rationale, could another court compel a
mother to "lie still" for fetal surgery against her will, or to accept the
risk of diagnostic steps to decide whether a surgical solution existed?
Could the compelling interest of the state be interpreted—even at
the previable stage—as permitting the court to order and enforce
"no smoking" or "no drinking" policies on the part of all pregnant
women during early pregnancy, or would the issue of "viability" be
the deciding factor? Just where will the line be drawn in balancing
the rights of the fetus on the one hand and those of the mother?
And just where does the responsibility of the physician rest to expose
these issues when they appear on the clinical scene?

One other point deserving attention was the court's deference to
medical authority—in this particular case, over the objections of the

family. As noted by Finamore in the *American Journal of Law and Medicine* (1983) such deference to authority and medical technology may have detrimental consequences, "granting such deference can devalue the patient's rights." Moreover, what happens when medical authority is divided on an issue—to whom ought the court listen?

Finally (and coincidentally with this case), comes a report of our Canadian colleagues, who have been reviewing that nation's position regarding euthanasia, aiding suicide, and the cessation of treatment. Additional discussions of their conclusions will be included in subsequent case reports. Suffice it to say that they have strongly recommended that deference to medical recommendations be granted in situations similar to those reported here. However, where disputes of medical recommendations take place, they call for court intrusion—as in the instance of their now-famous "Dawson Case" in British Columbia. Something similar seems predictable for the United States.

5

Traditional Malpractice Problems

All of the following problems have cropped up repeatedly in the past and will, no doubt, occur in the future. Some stem from "judgment calls"; others from "system failure." Those involved understandably are not eager to relive their mistakes; none wants to talk about them even in the abstract. But talk about them we must, doing our utmost to detect that etiologic element that might be modified or avoided in the future. And, increasingly, aggressive claims management, i.e., a willingness to reach out and settle quietly and quickly, is called for.

Section 7.   Doing Too Little—Failure to Diagnose
Section 8.   Doing Too Much—Excessive Efforts
Section 9.   Surgical Complications
Section 10.   Claims without "Medical" Fault
Section 11.   Hospital-Based Quality Review
Section 12.   Analysis of Recent Losses

SECTION 7

Doing Too Little—Failure to Diagnose

Case 1. G. O., a 57-year-old white male, had a ten-year history of increasing dyspnea, orthopnea, and angina. His family physician referred him to a cardiologist, who recommended diagnostic evaluation with an eye toward an eventual cardiac by-pass. He was hospi-

40

talized for catheterization and angiographic studies, which appeared to go well. However, after the procedures, suddenly he was noted to have a decreased pulse and blood pressure in his left leg with progressive discomfort there. Vascular surgical consultation was obtained immediately, although no precipitating cause of the problem was identified. He was operated on for an embolic episode, but already some permanent damage had occurred and eventually a portion of his forefoot was amputated.

Subsequently, an employee of the hospital, who had not been involved with the actual procedure, discussed the situation with the patient and allegedly told him that something must have gone wrong or been overlooked, and that appropriate tests had not been carried out. As a consequence, the patient assumed that negligence had occurred and consulted an attorney, who instituted a suit against both the physician and the hospital. After subpoenaing the hospital records and taking depositions from the staff, the attorney recommended dropping the case because of the excellent documentation in the medical records of what had actually transpired. Of note was the fact that the details of the hospital employee's accusations were not revealed to the defendant physician or his attorney until after the case had been discarded, serving as yet another example of a possible adversarial relationship between the hospital's insurance carrier and the physician's carrier.

Case 2. T. K., a 37-year-old white male, had always been in good health except for a tendency toward obesity. He carried 278 pounds on a 5'10'' frame. Employed as a truck driver he frequently lifted 50- to 100-pound boxes. During one such lift, T. K. experienced the onset of pain in his upper back and left shoulder, which gradually increased and persisted so that he sought medical attention in a nearby emergency room. There his vital signs were found to be normal except for a blood pressure of 182/102, with heart sounds being interpreted as entirely normal. Both an EKG and chest film were within normal limits. During the visit, T. K. displayed considerable unhappiness over the amount of time (in fact less than 30 minutes) he had to wait before being seen and tested. He left unexpectedly and without stopping at the desk to pay his bill. Later that night, while he was sitting at home watching TV, the back pain became more intense and now included excruciating anterior chest pain and dyspnea. He was finally taken back to the emergency room, where shortly after arrival he was pronounced dead. A suit was filed alleging that his death was due to lack of appropriate diagnostic techniques. Fortunately, the medical record spoke for itself and the claim was dismissed.

Case 3.   P. B., a 27-year-old multipara, entered the labor room with her fifth term pregnancy. She had no complications during her current pregnancy or any of her prior ones. Labor progressed sluggishly; over the four hours of the evening, she was examined on several occasions by both her physician and the labor room staff, who detected no observable problems. In contrast to two previous labors, however, no fetal monitoring equipment was employed. The patient subsequently alleged that when she asked a labor room nurse why none was used, she was told, "Dr. X doesn't believe in electronic fetal monitoring."

About 40 minutes after her physician's last visit, P. B. was recognized as having significant fetal bradycardia and almost immediately an uneventful Cesarean section was performed, with delivery of a 3,740-gram female. Two years later the child showed enough evidence of delayed development and neuromuscular spasticity to prompt the filing of a lawsuit. The allegation was negligence on the physician's part. Depositions taken confirmed the patient's allegation of the labor room nurse's statement, but other details in the record failed to reveal any negligence in the technique of fetal monitoring employed. Nonetheless, a final settlement to the plaintiff was made as a result of the episode.

Discussion

Among other points, these cases serve to illustrate the emerging problems of allegations of failure to diagnose. This category of malpractice case is replacing the traditional "inadequate surgical treatment" as the most common cause of liability actions. It should also be noted that two of the cases were precipitated by intraprofessional disputes between physicians and some hospital staff members. This problem, too, is recognized nationally as an increasingly significant one as different groups vie for greater status and turf—and the patient (consumer) is asked to settle the matter. Leaders of the professions simply must get together to set a course to resolve such dilemmas or the situation will only grow worse.

Recently, some professional programs aimed at helping physicians better cope with professional liability problems have been published. Dorothy Rasinski, M.D., J.D., with 20 years' experience as an internist on the one hand and a medical/legal expert on the other, outlines the "nine R's of malpractice prevention" in the May 1982 issue of the American Society of Internal Medicine's *Internist:*

1. rapport—establish good relationship with patients, relatives, hospital and office staff;

2. rationale—use an acceptable plan of diagnosis and treatment;

3. records—document the performance of that plan;

4. remarks—avoid offhand and gratuitous as well as "silent comments";

5. Rx's—register contraindications, interactions, and allergies to drugs;

6. *res ipsa loquitur*—if the matter speaks for itself, make prompt and adequate restitution;

7. respect—show respect for the patient's wishes, background, and culture;

8. results—itemize the possibilities in advance, both good and bad;

9. risks—discuss risks fully preceding an informed consent.

In her summary, Rasinski cautions physicians "to practice the best medicine at all times; to treat the patient with care, concern, humaneness and respect and to prepare and maintain careful records."

Also of interest is Attorney Melvin Belli's August 23, 1982, article in *Medical Economics* outlining what keeps him from accepting a plaintiff's case. He describes situations where patients seek revenge, where they've ignored advice, where they've misunderstood instructions, where emergency situations supervene, or simply, where bad results have occurred without negligence—but he checks the record to assure the validity of the patient's position first. Finally, Brenner and Jesse's contribution to the May 1982 issue of *Patient Care* outlines how your hospital's present quality assurance program can, at no additional cost, be used to minimize the risks of malpractice allegations against you and your colleagues.

As might be suspected, none of the three articles cited above outlines any simple magical cure for the malpractice crisis at hand; quite to the contrary, each stresses that all of us should in our day-to-day behavior do what we can to treat our patients with care, and not look to others to try to solve our problems.

What You Can Do

In your hospital or in your office, is there a real opportunity for staff to discuss possible intraprofessional disagreements? Can the unit assistant, the floor nurse, or the office receptionist bring up points of concern? When was the last time one did?

In your office, do you have a clearly specified policy about what to do when patients seek second opinions or desire to change physicians to seek additional consultation? Does your staff comply, and how can you be sure?

In your hospital, what is being done to try to head off otherwise inevitable conflicts between the physicians' carriers and the hospital's carrier when both are parties to a common suit? Has the issue ever reached the discussion phase with your Joint Conference Committee? If so, what, if anything, happened? Does your medical staff know about it?

SECTION 8

Doing Too Much—Excessive Efforts

Case 1. E. N., a 31-year-old para 2 gravida 3, had visited her previous obstetrician after missing a period and detecting the usual symptoms of pregnancy. All went well, with an estimated date of confinement calculated for mid-November. By early October, however, fundal height and uterine size seemed compatible with delivery date of one month earlier. Planning to be away for some ten days, the obstetrician—with the encouragement of the patient—arranged for elective induction of labor. Premature twins were born, one of whom was diagnosed several years later as suffering from consequences of perinatal hypoxia with subsequent "brain damage." A negligence action was successful, based, in part, upon the physician's failure to diagnose the presence of twins, but to a more significant extent upon his intervening when such intervention was not deemed to be necessary.

Case 2. P. P., a 52-year-old woman, had suffered persistent back pain subsequent to "stepping off a school bus the wrong way." Treated initially as a "Labor and Industries case," she had back (disc) surgery on at least four, and possibly as many as six, different occasions, all apparently by different physicians and all without significant relief of symptoms. Eventually consulting yet another physician, she specified allergies to at least four drugs: penicillin, aspirin, codeine, and sulphonamides. Nonetheless, in an effort to manage her back pain, she was given Robaxin, Percodan, and Doriden, the latter two of which she also had obtained from other doctors as well. Increasingly dependent on drugs, and continuing to suffer back symptoms, she allegedly became depressed at the cessation of the Percodan, and took a lethal overdose of a combination of acetaminophen and salicylate. A successful negligence action was instituted by her family against her last physician for prescribing excessive and inappropriate medications. Interestingly, no comparable actions were brought against either those who had operated on her repeatedly, or those who were her other sources of narcotics.

Case 3. S. W., a 47-year-old business executive under considerable strain as his firm merged with a conglomerate, noted some transient substernal discomfort while watching professional football on Sunday TV. When the symptoms abated within 15 minutes, during which interval he had taken some milk, S. W. decided to defer any other remedial action and arranged to visit his physician the next day. At that time, the remainder of the history and the physical examination were found to be normal. A weekend tennis player and three-times-a-week jogger, S. W.'s weight was slightly below average for his size; his vital signs and blood pressure were normal; EKG, chest x-ray, and cardiac enzymes were all normal. Nevertheless, a cardiac consultation and then heart catheterization were arranged. During the procedure "something went wrong"; the result: air embolism and death.

Post-mortem cardiac findings were limited to minimal atherosclerosis with no major vascular or valvular pathology. Although the major criterion for the six-figure settlement was based upon the technologic disaster, a contributory issue was voiced by three different consultants to the plaintiff: "Why was the cardiac catheterization performed in the first place?" The answer: "Because, apparently, the patient had insisted on it—not because of any clear-cut medical indications."

Discussion

Each of these cases illustrates a physician's inappropriate response to a patient's complaint or request. In each instance, the doctor's response was "to do something"—to induce labor, to prescribe medication, to conduct a test. Through the retrospectoscope, each doctor did too much or moved too soon.

In most instances of medical malpractice, just the opposite has occurred; the doctor is charged with failing to do enough—failing to get an informed consent, failing to carry out appropriate diagnostic tests, failing to follow the patient's course, failing to look for drug interactions, or failing to operate effectively. Certainly on a percentage basis, these failures to act far outweigh in frequency doing too much. A maxim of the profession is that "the road to medical hell is paved with errors of omission." According to conventional wisdom, one simply doesn't travel that road by doing too much. Yet in this era of cost containment, third-party carriers and their representatives, as well as anxious and often well-informed patients themselves, the practitioner is caught in a bind of wanting to do everything indicated, reasonable, appropriate, or possible, but not wanting to put the patient at risk of injury or excessive costs. Many times the physician's action is, in fact, a judgment call.

As noted by Hilfiker in his exemplary essay, "Facing Our Ethical Choices," on the chronically ill, the physician is in a Catch-22 position between doing too much and doing too little, and oftentimes without adequate professional guidelines (Hilfiker 1983).

Section 7 emphasized significant errors of omission; these continue to constitute a major area where remedial actions can help prevent malpractice allegations. Errors of commission, however, remain significant contributors to the overall problem. Writing gratuitous comments in charts ridiculing fellow practitioners' therapeutic strategies or casting aspersions on the patient's character, for example, can be devastating to efforts at justice. Derogatory verbal comments that are easily overheard by patients or relatives and able to be captured out of context are notorious for their detrimental effects. Such professional jousting should be discouraged. And, as is illustrated here,—doing too much can set the stage for something to go wrong.

Admittedly, many problems occur when the doctor is simply responding conscientiously to the patient's complaints, but these complaints may be exaggerated or even factitious. No one said it better than Richard Asher, who developed his now-famous "Munchhausen's Syndrome" to describe patients who almost boastfully fabricate symptoms and signs to feign illness. Physician after physician has been duped by such characters, and the outcome can be disastrous. Emphasizing the need for professional skepticism in this interplay is Meadow's description of the consequences of "Munchhausen's Syndrome by Proxy"—a mother purposely deceives the doctor about her child's condition. Her six-year-old child "endured 13 months away from school, five months in the hospital, one month of intravenous fluids, and the following procedures: two barium meals, two IVPs, skeletal survey, brain scan, two lumbar punctures, two electroencephalograms, bone biopsy, kidney biopsy, and skin biopsy. In addition, he had endoscopy of the upper gastrointestinal tract and more than 120 venipunctures!" During the same period of time, the child received at least 28 different drugs, and at the time of discovery of the deception was being considered for plasmaphoresis.

While no allegation of malpractice was made in this particular case and while contributory negligence by the mother would certainly be cited as a defense, such episodes can set the stage for errors to occur (as they usually do) during elaborate investigations or treatment. Too much or too little is a difficult judgment call. It warrants professional skepticism as well as dedication on the part of the physician.

What You Can Do

In your hospital, is there any concerted effort to review admissions, not simply for prolonged stay but for evidence of too much investigation? If any significant deviations were found, how would they be addressed? Is careful review given to the indications for elective surgery against group-determined norms?

In your office, how do you handle the patient who demands clearly excessive laboratory investigations, or excessive medication? In your history taking, do you make it a practice to check out complaints which led to repetitive operative procedures or prolonged courses of excessive medications?

When confronted with an apparent insoluble diagnostic dilemma in an otherwise healthy-appearing individual, do you seek out one more test ("let's try a liver battery") or do you employ other options, such as a second opinion or the passage of time? The choices are legion and difficult; excessive action itself can be fraught with bad consequences.

SECTION 9

Surgical Complications

Case 1.   M. B., a 68-year-old white male, had been an insulin-dependent diabetic for many years. He had developed severe peripheral vascular disease with extensive ulcer problems on both lower extremities with chronic osteomyelitis on the left. Unresponsive to continued medical management, he was scheduled for amputation after full discussion of the alternatives with him and his relatives. Carefully prepared, he was brought into the operating room and positioned for surgery. Despite following traditional routine steps, the responsible surgeon proceeded to amputate the wrong lower extremity; naturally a financial settlement followed.

Case 2.   T. M., a 2½-year-old female, had been recognized early in infancy as having congenital heart disease; the symptoms had been controlled by medical management during the first two years of life. More recently, severe prolonged episodes of respiratory illness and an actual reduction in weight suggested that definitive operative repair ought to be undertaken. In preparation for such procedure, clarification of the details of the cardiac lesion was sought by way of cardiac catheterization via a peripheral radial artery. Despite an apparently uneventful procedure, postoperatively T. M. developed evidence of embolization in the arm with subsequent loss of tissue and eventual loss of the digital portion of her hand. A financial settlement was arranged.

Case 3.   P. T., a 31-year-old female, had sought sterilization; the surgery was performed via laparoscopy. The procedure appeared to go well until the anesthesiologist recognized a failing blood pressure; emergency laparotomy revealed perforation of the abdominal aorta. Eventually a repair was accomplished, but not until after extensive complications (temporary renal shutdown, prolonged hospital stay, etc.) had occurred; again, a financial settlement was arranged.

Case 4. T. G., a 34-year-old male, had a long-standing problem with severe obesity, which was seemingly resistant to all forms of medical management. Arrangements were undertaken to perform an intestinal by-pass procedure at his community hospital. The operation was completed with difficulty only after a prolonged period of anesthesia, and the postoperative period was complicated by atelectasis, pneumonia, and apparent anastemotic leak, peritonitis, sepsis, and prolonged hospitalization with a secondary abdominal procedure. The patient suffered considerable discomfort, and was awarded a financial settlement.

Discussion

Each of the four preceding cases exemplifies a complication associated with surgery; in toto, such complications account for a large component of malpractice claims. In each of the instances cited, through peer review of the details involved led to a conclusion that the problem was clearly avoidable: the first, by strict adherence to called-for OR policy; the second, by cautious positional management of the involved extremity, with careful postoperative monitoring; the third, by way of more thorough preparation of the laparoscopist; and the fourth, at the very least, by conduct of the procedure in other than a small rural hospital. Many other comparable cases could be recounted from throughout Washington State or other states; while the details may differ, some general inferences hold remarkably constant:

1. In many cases, basic doctor-patient communication has been at fault. Patient expectations may be distorted, and under those circumstances any complication is perceived as a complete surprise. Personal trust in the surgeon may be missing. Attention to the details of avoiding such complications in advance by participating physicians, surgeons, and the entire hospital staff ought to help modify the extent of the problem.

2. All too often hindsight suggests that detailed training for the procedure itself and careful attention to handling its possible complications has not been implemented. Again and again, what should have been routine has been overlooked; frequently the OR team

has never run through a "disaster drill"; on occasion, the staff nurses may not have been trained in dealing with complications of a particular surgical procedure. Again, better pre-op, intra-op, and post-op communications by the responsible surgeon are imperative.

3. Frequently, the delicate balance between the surgeon's necessary "courage of convictions" on the one hand and "humbleness titre" on the other is not maintained in trying to deal with patient problems. All too often, while extensive medical consultation has been fully taken care of, appropriate surgical consultation is not sought. Here, too, the opportunity for surgeons to work together in advance would seem worth taking advantage of.

4. Many hospital peer review programs, while up and running considerably more effectively than they were ten years ago, still experience problems. Credential reviews of initial or continuing staff privileges often become pro forma. Under some circumstances, when deficiencies are detected, no action follows; and when it does, it is only after considerable time has elapsed. An assertive, active credentials review program must be undertaken at the level of the hospital—and now is the time.

5. Quite candidly, effective joint hospital-physician risk management programs in many hospitals seem conspicuous by their absence. In their respective enthusiasm for pointing fingers and placing blame, both parties conceivably overlook the necessity of trying to identify and resolve potential patient care problems before they arise. The recently adopted "Quality Assurance Programs" required by the Joint Commission on Accreditation of Hospitals may help to resolve the problems. Regardless, more participation by individual physicians and by medical staff would go a long way toward implementing programs to minimize allegations of malpractice. The hospital and the doctor simply cannot go on as silent partners in trying to resolve the ever-increasing issues of professional liability.

What You Can Do

In your hospital, is there careful review of all complications of surgery aimed not simply at establishing blame, but at future prevention?

Does your Credentials Committee review each application for initial and/or continuing staff privileges as if any oversights on their part might put the entire hospital staff in significant jeopardy? According to the courts in New Jersey, infringement by one individual *can* jeopardize the whole organization.

Does your Credentials Committee reinvent the wheel when considering criteria for staff privileges, or do they take advantage of extensive experiences gathered elsewhere? Have you actually served on, or participated in, any joint hospital-physician efforts at risk management? If not, what can you do to correct that?

In your county, do you use a county-wide medical society-developed application form for hospital staff privileges, which can be fully corroborated to assist all of the individual hospitals in saving time and effort while achieving accuracy?

SECTION 10

Claims Recovery without "Medical" Fault

Case 1. H. S., a 35-year-old mother of three, developed an acute illness manifested by slight fever, lethargy, and weakness, followed by paralysis in both lower extremities. Some three weeks earlier, her youngest child had received Sabin (oral) polio vaccine. At that time H. S. said that she had previously been vaccinated. Moreover she read in detail and signed the extensive informed consent form prepared by the county health department prior to her child's immunization. Although it was never precisely proved that she had actually contracted polio or that, if she had, it was caused by the vaccine virus, and although she had been fully informed, both the manufacturer of the vaccine and the county health department (but not the physician) were found to be culpable, and a large award followed.

Case 2. J. C., a 56-year-old moderately obese woman, had noted blood in her stool. Her physician confirmed active bleeding and made a diagnosis of villous adenoma of the bowel. Brought to the operating room for surgical removal of the adenoma, J. C. experienced no problems whatever until the induction of the spinal anesthesia, when she sustained an abrupt cardiac arrest. She then lapsed into a coma which persisted without evidence of recovery of neurologic function. Despite what appeared to be almost instantaneous recognition and appropriate treatment of the arrest, and despite a lack of evidence that the administration of anesthesia was faulty, the plaintiff's relatives claimed inadequate information, and received a settlement of more than half a million dollars from the hospital, physician, and surgeon.

Case 3.   W. A., a three-year-old boy, underwent definitive surgical repair of complicated congenital heart problems. Unfortunately, he continued to do poorly and after a year was judged to be a candidate for an internal pacemaker. One was inserted with good results for some six months, but then it began to fail. He was returned to the operating room for exploration, testing, and replacement of the pulse generator. Afterwards, while he was being prepared for transfer to the recovery room, the Doppler monitor apparently became dislodged. Although the EKG remained stable, showing normal pacemaker functions, the arterial pulsation was lost. External cardiac massage was initiated immediately, but the effort was complicated by extubation of an airway during subsequent chest x-ray. Despite all efforts at treatment, the child sustained severe neurologic damage, and a 30-year structured settlement was arranged.

Discussion

On occasion there are instances where, at least on the surface, the individual physician or the "community" of physicians appear to have little opportunity to alter an outcome. Thus, in Case 1, the individual physician had sought a patient's history and obtained the appropriate consent; as an individual he could have done little else. Perhaps as a group, we ought to be pushing harder for some type of legislative remedy; unfortunately, each proposed solution in turn appears to create its own set of undesirable consequences. The "back to nature" movement combined with national publicity about problems with pertussis vaccine, polio vaccine, and flu vaccine are all serving to dissuade parents from obtaining appropriate immunization for their children, frequently despite a state's requirement of immunization to attend school. The wise physician will want to document any instances of parental noncompliance. For those who do comply, the physician will note the fact that he or she has discussed the possibility of vaccine complication with the parent and that the parent has agreed to proceed with the immunization.

In spite of extensive examination and analysis, Case 2 remains an enigma: no recognizable fault was uncovered with either the anesthesia or the resuscitative efforts. While nothing specific surfaced, the review procedure itself did serve to tighten a few practices in the involved hospital which appeared to need tightening.

Similarly, examination of Case 3 proved to be a particularly frustrating experience. The monitoring procedure was complex and complementary and appeared to work well, except for a momentary mechanical failure, i.e., the Doppler became dislodged (as opposed to someone dislodging it). Again, careful procedural review followed the incident, to the benefit of future patients and physicians.

What You Can Do

In your office, have you reviewed your policies and practices on immunization? Tetanus boosters for adults? Live versus dead polio vaccine? Consent forms? Are you in line with your state's standards of practice?

In your hospital, when mistakes occur—and despite the best intentions they occur everywhere—do they prompt an "incident report" and a thorough review of the incident? Is the medical staff appropriately involved and does it provide leadership in the process? Has incident reporting been formally incorporated into your hospital's quality assurance plan to assure appropriate immunity?

Some components of malpractice are so unlikely to occur that they require insurance for protection against them. However, many components are quite common and can be eliminated by individual and corporate group activities of physicians. Do your part; support the risk management program.

SECTION 11

Hospital-Based Quality Review

Case 1. E. W., a 71-year-old male, had complained of increasing lower extremity weakness, inability to stand or walk, and severe discomfort in his feet because of coldness. Clinical examination and an-giographic studies confirmed severe atherosclerosis with luminal narrowing, particularly just proximal to the aortic bifurcation, but also throughout both legs. He underwent an uncomplicated aortic femoral by-pass, but then had an especially stormy postoperative course. He experienced multiple emboli to the lower extremities, loss of several toes, temporary renal shutdown, several emboli to the lungs, and at least one significant cerebral ischemic episode. E. W. subse-quently brought suit alleging inadequate technical postoperative management. His case was heard by a Claims Review Panel, which advised compromise; a settlement in excess of $200,000 was reached.

Case 2.   A. M., a 33-year-old para 2 gravida 3, had an apparently normal pregnancy. As she went into labor, however, she began to complain of a headache. At that time, her urine showed significant protein, and her blood pressure was reported as being dramatically elevated. Despite these ominous signs no agressive management for toxemia took place until almost eight hours after the delivery of her child. By that time she had apparently sustained irremedial damage and despite heroic efforts both locally and at the tertiary care hos-pital, she died. The final award to her family exceeded $1,000,000.

Case 3.   P. R., an obese 26-year-old para 2 gravida 3, had passed her estimated delivery date by some three weeks without any evi-dence of labor. Since there had been no problems during pregnancy and because clinical examination was entirely normal, she agreed to have her labor induced. All went well (including fetal monitoring) until delivery was imminent, when it was recognized that the baby was "small." Arriving at 2,180 grams with Apgars of 3 and 5, the baby developed severe respiratory distress syndrome and eventually was determined to be developmentally impaired. An action was brought citing negligence in the advice given to induce labor. A set-tlement of more than $50,000 followed.

Discussion

Each of these cases represents large awards during the period of 1976–81 in Washington State. A total of 711 claims were closed during that period by the then-sponsored carrier. In the detailed report covering that period (Aetna's Annual Report to WSMA, 1981), 8 cases involving induction of labor had triggered settlements in excess of $50,000 apiece; 12 cases of retropubic uterine suspension for stress incontinence, 9 cases of surgical "mismanagement," 11 of aortic femoral by-pass problems, 10 of inadequate use of mid-forceps, and 6 cholecystectomies precipitated comparable awards. The authors of the report suggest, and one can't help but agree, that these cases and other "high losers" warrant careful review by all physicians to ensure that more appropriate management is now taking place.

To that end, the WSMA developed a series of "Risk Management Review Units" to help each local hospital's medical staff look into those clinical problems associated with large malpractice awards, and to modify any shortcomings detected. Initially, these review units were aimed at easily identifiable issues where little or no professional controversy was likely to occur. Subsequently, the program has been expanded to include more complicated and controversial topics. And, in the meantime, specialty societies have also been alerted to "high loss problem areas" in their specialties and urged to develop appropriate continuing education efforts. A detailed description of the Risk Management Program and the component review units is found in the Appendix.

All WSMA members across the state were urged to cooperate in this venture. Information is collected on the local scene and is intended to remain there. Provided the data are collected in collaboration with the hospital's quality assurance activities, the results are not subject to discovery. A challenge to such immunity was rejected by the courts. Remember: if episodes resulting in allegations of malpractice can be reduced, it will mean that patient care has been improved.

What You Can Do

In your hospital, will you and your colleagues insist that the Risk Management Review Units be implemented? Can you expect to get reports of the outcome of those reviews? Can you count on some changes in behavior to follow, or will the report simply be filed?

In your state, how do physicians determine if each medical staff is discharging its review obligations? It is in your own best interest to make sure.

SECTION 12

Analysis of Recent Losses

Case 1. M. P., a 56-year-old woman, had recurrent bouts of right upper quadrant pain. Investigation led to a diagnosis of "chronic cholecystitis and gall stones." Found to be otherwise normal, she was scheduled for elective cholecystectomy, which she tolerated without incident. Three days later, however, she spiked a fever and complained of right upper quadrant pain and some increasing dyspnea. Almost immediately, a clinical and laboratory evaluation followed, leading to a diagnosis of wound infection and possible abscess and/ or peritonitis. Prompt re-exploration followed, with drainage of an early abscess. Antibiotic therapy was instituted.

M. P. recovered slowing, remaining in the hospital for some twelve days prior to discharge. Subsequently a charge of negligence was brought, but a careful review of the case by consultants eventually led to the dropping of the allegation. During the review of the case, it was determined that significantly more postoperative infections than would have been predicted were occurring at that hospital; through the efforts of all parties involved, the rate of infections dropped to baseline in the ensuing year.

Case 2. S. F., a 17-year-old male, was brought to an emergency room because of a sudden onset of vomiting and increasing obtundation. Other than recently recovering from chicken pox, S. F. had always been relatively healthy. Suspected of having Reye's Syndrome ("hepatic-cerebral failure"), S. F. was admitted to the intensive care unit. Some confusion followed as to which physician was to be in charge and under whose orders he came. Appropriate standard therapy was eventually started, but to no avail; the patient died. There was a lawsuit based on the premise that interprofessional communication had failed and that inadequate therapeutic efforts had been mobilized. Again, when consultants reviewed the case they disagreed as to the standard of care which should have been applied to the patient. A settlement resulted.

Case 3.   T. W., a 27-year-old male, had had more than a decade of a persistent problem of obesity. Many therapeutic efforts had been undertaken; none appeared to have been of any benefit. Finally, T. W. sought an intestinal by-pass procedure. He received thorough preoperative evaluation, and signed appropriate consent forms. The surgery seemed to go well, yet suddenly the patient died postoperatively, suspected of having an acute pulmonary embolus. Detailed review of the case left a number of unanswered questions regarding the informed consent (which had been obtained with both the patient and his wife present), the anesthetic technique employed, and the procedure itself. When a malpractice action was instituted, the involved defendants claimed that their procedures had been "above reproach." Some out of state experts, however, took serious exception to the indications for therapy, as well as to the techniques involved. A large settlement eventually followed.

Case 4.   H. H., a 13-year-old male traveling from out of state with his parents, suddenly became ill. He developed rapid onset of nausea, vomiting, and obvious systemic toxicity. Taken to an emergency room, he was examined thoroughly and suspected of having a systemic infection. After cultures of blood, stool, urine, and cerebral spinal fluid were taken, he was admitted for antibiotic therapy less than two hours after arriving in the emergency room. Despite all efforts at therapy and resuscitative heroics, he died within four hours; his blood culture grew out pneumococcus.

Previously H. H. had had a post-trauma splenectomy, which had been recorded in the admission work-up, but which had not been recognized as a significant risk to sepsis. Nor had it been documented that the parents were warned at the time of the splenectomy that H. H. would be at sizeable risk of sepsis with pneumococcus. A malpractice action was directed not at the treating physicians in the emergency room or at the hospital, but rather at the site of the initial splenectomy, alleging failure to inform as its basis.

Discussion

The above cases cited typify a range of problems associated with malpractice. The frequency of claims appears to be climbing in Washington; the cost of each case also appears to be skyrocketing.

WSMA's previous sponsored carrier (Aetna), for example, compiled a study of all cases reported to Aetna over the period January 1981 through July 1982, which carried a $100,00 or greater reserve. During those 18 months, it was found that 75 (out of a total of 450) cases had been reported. The mean figure for these 75 cases alone was $243,000 each, for a grand total of $18.2 million. When one compares that figure with the average loss of $33,000 for 1,039 claims closed between 1976 and 1980, one senses the degree of escalation which has ensued. It seems clearly to be a variation on the relatively constant 22 percent increment which had occurred between 1963 and 1977.

In addition to pinpointing probable heavy losses, Aetna also shared with WSMA its most recent closed-claims data up through December 1980. Those data encompassed the four-year totals of the 1,039 cases referred to above. Dissecting each case into specified variables and then determining correlations, Aetna found that, when the time lapse between the incident and its disposition was looked at, early reporting of the incident and aggressive resolution of the problem proved to be beneficial. For example, if disposition was achieved in less than three months, the costs (when there were any) averaged only $4,400 per case; if the disposition time fell between four and six months, it rose to $14,800; from six months to a year, $17,800; from one to two years, $55,000; and between two and three years, $75,000! The clear conclusion: prompt reporting of the incident to the carrier, combined with expeditious claims management, expedites settlement to the patient or family and reduces costs for the physician and the carrier.

Despite much effort to publicize the absolute necessity of documenting informed consents in the records, it was discovered that some 24 percent of the 1,039 medical records involved failed to have an appropriately completed informed consent in the chart. In 1976, WSMA had prepared and made available an acceptable form; to date it has proven uniformly effective when used correctly. Imagine, however, your reaction were you to attend a medical staff meeting at a hospital within your county, say, in the spring of 1982, and hear a debate among the medical staff members as to whether using informed consent forms should be required. The doctors at that hospital would be actively exposing other physicians to needless and sizeable lawsuits. Do you know the policy within your hospital about documentation of informed consent?

At the same time, the closed-claim analysis revealed—in parallel with HEW's 1973 Commission on Medical Malpractice—that some 45 percent of the cases were judged "legally meritorious" by the carrier and/or its consultants. In actuality, some 66 percent evidenced at least a degree of professional negligence, but, in a number of instances there appeared to be no causal relationship between the negligence and the detrimental outcome.

For the skeptic, such findings should stress that a "let's clean up our act" response is appropriate. But it is necessary to go one step further. As a consequence of mandatory reporting of awards in excess of $30,000 each, 90 cases of malpractice losses were transmitted to the Medical Disciplinary Board and carefully reviewed by that Board and its consultants. Among those 90 cases not a single one was judged to reflect on the physician's behavior warranting efforts to lift the physician's license or privileges. Certainly, individual instances of negligence were obvious, but no pattern of unprofessional behavior developed. In contrast to expectations no easily identifiable "bad apples" were found. As an aside, one would also note that, while the insurance carriers reported 90 cases for review by the Medical Disciplinary Board, the state's county medical societies and hospitals reported only three instances of altered staff membership status in compliance with the mandatory reporting regulations. Does that mean that only three instances occurred of alterations in staff privileges? Or does it mean something else?

Again allegations of negligence during the diagnostic process itself were found in 32 percent of the 1,039 closed claims, with simple delay explaining 119, or 36 percent. Still other conclusions from this closed-claims study served to help formulate a Risk Management Program. Fortunately, with the emergence of WSMA's new sponsored carrier (Physicians Insurance Company), WSMA continues to receive the cooperation of four of the state's other carriers—Aetna, CNA, Group Health, and the University of Washington. Closed-claims data are being totaled from all five sources to develop a more accurate and more comprehensive data base from which to build our epidemiologic understanding and subsequent prevention program. Let your carrier know you support such cooperation; without summary data we will revert to the blind again leading the blind. With such co-operation, many detected deficits ought to be correctable.

What You Can Do

In your hospital, does your Executive Committee or Joint Conference Committee ever seek to determine what, if any, financial losses have occurred (doctor or hospital related) and then take steps to avoid the causative problem from recurring in the future?

In your office or in your hospital, has there been a concerted effort to detect potential incidents (or unhappy patients) by your staff so that early reporting, prompt investigation, and the construction of a defense or a just settlement can follow. Your staff can be of enormous help in this regard.

In your hospital, what was the outcome of the last audit of surgical charts for the presence of a signed informed consent? Are you sure one was ever done? Remember, it's your premium dollar that's at risk if we continue to see 24 percent of our closed claims in the state of Washington continue with this element of negligence. It can and does serve as a blank check on our combined reserves. With peer pressure, persistence, and the strong support of your anesthesiologists, the problem can be eliminated.

6

Damaged Babies

Without doubt, damaged babies are the number one medical malpractice concern of the 1980s. Infants born with severe deficits or those who develop them postnatally but who nonetheless survive are enormously expensive for society to maintain. Since someone has to pay, one method seems to be to attack the delivery process and its many uncertainties. The result is that the fastest rising premiums belong to obstetricians, who respond with more and more "defensive" medicine. This scenario may seem oversimplified and one-sided. Clearly, there have been real disasters in the past when mother and infant were needlessly subjected to risks. Sometimes it has been the physician at fault; at other times, societal pressure for twilight sleep was responsible; and at still others, the physical facilities themselves or unsanitary conditions proved critical. Looking at today through the spectacles of yesteryear permits identification of steps which can be taken to minimize, if not eliminate, many but not all hazards of childbirth and delivery. On the horizon looms the dilemma of how we are to manage the seriously deformed infant and all of the associated problems—while trying to avoid assigning blame, if none is appropriate.

61

SECTION 13

Problems with Pregnancy

Case 1. R. J., a 26-year-old married female, had been taking birth control pills for at least three years without complications. Intending to start her family, she ceased the medication in January and sought obstetrical consultation in mid-March, at which time pregnancy was confirmed. Care proved routine until late August when contractions and spotting began; this was followed by a physical examination and administration of pitocin, with delivery of a 4 lb. 11 oz. infant who rapidly succumbed to infantile respiratory distress syndrome (IRDS). A claim of negligence was brought on the grounds that in the absence of confirmatory evidence of the child's maturity, no induction of labor should have been instituted. Unfortunately, there was no clear evidence in the chart of the estimated date of confinement (EDC) or of physical or laboratory confirmation of the child's maturity, thus making the case non-defensible in the opinion of consultants. A significant settlement resulted.

Case 2. D. M., a 30-year-old married pregnant female, was referred by her physician to an obstetrical consultant during her third trimester in mid-January; he was to manage her delivery. Her EDC was late February. On the basis of his physical examination of the patient, plus her lack of recollection of either her last menstrual period or her first missed period—"I can't be sure"—the obstetrician proceeded to schedule her for an elective Cesarean section. The resultant "premature infant," weighing significantly less than 2,500 grams (5 lbs. 8 oz.), rapidly developed respiratory distress and succumbed in less than 12 hours to infantile respiratory distress syndrome. Negligence was alleged against the obstetrician for failing to adequately determine the maturity of the infant before proceeding with the Cesarean section; on the basis of the facts of the case, a substantial settlement was recommended by consultants and made.

Case 3. W. P., an adult-onset diabetic, para 1 gravida 2, had been followed through her second pregnancy without any significant problems; her EDC was mid-October. Despite mid-September x-ray evidence indicating lack of fetal maturity, an elective Cesarean section was carried out resulting in a 2,200-gram infant who rapidly succumbed to infantile respiratory distress syndrome. A year later, W. P. had an EDC of early December. She and her husband expressed reluctance to undergo early section for fear of a repeat premature infant. Because both chemical and x-ray data were indicative of adequate fetal maturity in early-November, an elective section was scheduled and was carried out in mid-November; it resulted in a 5,810-gram (12 lb. +) stillborn infant.

The combined experiences prompted the parents to bring a charge of professional negligence on the grounds that the first child was delivered too soon and the second too late. Despite obvious extenuating circumstances and somewhat divided professional opinion, the carrier deemed it wise to agree to a substantial settlement as opposed to risking the unpredictability of a jury trial.

Discussion

While it must be emphasized that these cases all transpired in the middle and late 1970s before the widespread availability of many new technologies to determine fetal maturity, the point must be made that just as the technology available then was not being used or was being used inappropriately, the same root problem persists today. Moreover, with the Cesarean section rate almost quadrupling in the past decade to more than 15 percent, the opportunity to intervene too early or too late has increased proportionately. However, this is only one element of what the insurance industry refers to as the "bad baby problem"—i.e., the end result of delivery is a severely damaged but surviving infant. The issue is of financial significance also. According to the National Association of Insurance Commission Closed Claim Study of 1975–78, the average indemnity loss for such cases climbed from $123,000 to $219,000 (a 78 percent increase) during the two-year interval of the study. That is almost eight times more than the average indemnity loss for all other cases and current evidence confirms a continuing escalation of awards.

What You Can Do

In your hospital, are your obstetrical department (obstetricians and family physicians) and your pediatric department aware of the enormity of the "bad baby problem"? Have they jointly with nursing and hospital administration sat down to review what mechanisms are in place to minimize the occurrence of these problems or to identify appropriate steps that might be instituted? Moreover, are they sure that any of their recommendations are actually being implemented?

As an example, are you certain that each infant is, in fact, tested for PKU and thyroid deficiency with the results reported back to the attending physician, and not simply filed in the hospital closet as was done on one occasion which resulted in a $1,000,000 negligence award?

Be as sure as you can that your medical staff is doing its utmost to eliminate both individual and system failure.

SECTION 14

More Pregnancy-Related Issues

Case 1. J. N., a 3,250-gram newborn female, was born after the apparently normal pregnancy of a healthy 29-year-old para 3 gravida 4. Labor had been uneventful and progressed to delivery in approximately five hours. The entire process took place in a hospital setting, with the mother having been seen by the attending physician on at least two occasions during her labor. Moreover, she and two other patients were under the supervision of an experienced obstetrical nurse.

At the time of delivery, the baby was noted to be unusually flaccid; her Apgar score was 2 at one and five minutes. Life-support measures were initiated promptly and carried out successfully; spontaneous respirations subsequently ensued, but the child's overall condition remained poor. Transferred to a referral institution, the child continued to do poorly. It was felt that significant CNS impairment resulting from intrauterine hypoxia was the cause of her problem. Unfortunately, a search of the labor room records failed to reveal any documentation of fetal heart monitoring. Both the nurse and the physician claimed that monitoring had been carried out, but the records failed to substantiate their position. During the case discussion in front of the Claims Review Panel, the point was made repeatedly that lack of such documentation makes defense extremely difficult. A settlement followed.

Case 2. T. B., a 2,785-gram male neonate, was delivered by an apparently healthy 25-year-old para 2 gravida 3 in a hospital setting. The pregnancy had been apparently normal; labor progressed without problems; electronic fetal monitoring was instituted after the membranes ruptured. Delivery with saddleblock anesthesia appeared to be uneventful, but the infant arrived with a low Apgar score at both one and five minutes. He responded poorly to immediate and prolonged respiratory assistance. Upon transfer to another institution, he continued to do poorly. The consulting physician, without having seen the labor room records, entered a note in the chart that the child's distressed condition was "clearly attributable to prolonged intrauterine hypoxia." He shared that opinion with the parents and with their legal counsel. Subsequently, the child was diagnosed as having developmental delay. Fortunately, the record at the hospital of delivery was adequately documented to contest the consultant physician's opinion. After considerable discussion the case was settled without payment.

Case 3. G. O., a 2,345-gram newborn female, was the product of a normal labor and delivery by an Rh-positive para 1 gravida 2 in a hospital setting. Found to be free of any detectable problems at 24 hours of age, the child was discharged home with the mother at 36 hours. At approximately 90 hours of age, the child was returned to the attending physician's office because she was noted to be increasingly jaundiced. At that time, the bilirubin level in the infant exceeded 32 milligrams percent, and the child was readmitted for exchange transfusion and elimination of the hyperbilirubinemic problem. Some two years later, however, an apparent developmental delay was ascribed to the neonatal episode of hyperbilirubinemia. In preparing the defense, it was discovered that there was no evidence in the chart anywhere—in the labor room record, delivery record, the mother's or the patient's chart—of any instructions whatever being provided to the mother when she was originally discharged from the hospital telling her what to feed the baby or what to look for in the way of symptoms. While no financial settlement followed, a prolonged debate ensued stemming from the obvious record deficit.

Case 4. S. W., a 1,895-gram female, the second of twins, was delivered by elective Cesarean section of a 31-year-old para 2 gravida

3 after an apparently normal pregnancy. The time of delivery had been made on calculations from the mother's last menstrual period; twins had not been expected. Both infants had trouble initiating respiratory efforts. The first twin responded rapidly to routine measures; the second (S. W.) responded poorly. After attempted stabilization, S. W. was transferred to a referral institution for continued therapy of the IRDS. By nine months of age, significant developmental delay was apparent. A claim was filed based on the position that the attending obstetrician had failed to use adequate methods for determining the estimated date of conception and the presence of twins, and therefore, had mis-scheduled the elective Cesarean section. A settlement followed.

Discussion

Some say that "damaged baby" problems usually involve only family physicians, obstetricians, and pediatricians. Others say that, in Washington State, for example, they are limited to only 80 of 120 state hospitals. In truth, they affect and will continue to affect all hospitals and all physicians via their professional liability premiums. For example, the primary reason for the 1982 request for a 371 percent increase in professional liability premiums by New York's Joint Underwriting Association was the problem posed by 30–35 "bad baby cases" waiting in the wings. In Washington, such cases rank number one in size of settlements, with an average almost ten times the $25–30,000 costs of other cases. A number of factors are involved.

In the 1950s and 1960s there was much publicity about the "unusually high" neonatal mortality rates in the United States. Since then much effort has been directed toward alleviating the problem, much technology has been applied to solving the dilemma. Today the situation is greatly improved, the neonatal mortality rate continues to fall, though the precise causes remain uncertain. Simultaneously, patient expectations have skyrocketed. Favorable outcomes seem taken for granted once the ogres of rubella and inherited illness are cast aside. Costs of hospital deliveries have also skyrocketed, as the costs stem from the search for safety. In addition, much press coverage has reinforced the belief that, if it is safe to deliver at home or in a birthing center with the help of a midwife, it must really be safe to deliver in a hospital with the help of a physician. When something goes wrong, somebody must have been negligent!

When a damaged baby is born, the reactions of parents are understandable, particularly when they are faced with the overwhelming costs of prolonged hospitalization and specialized care for the life of their impaired infant. In truth, some Cesarean sections are undertaken in the face of dubious determinations of maturity, and the decidedly premature infant develops IRDS and other complications as a result.

Although the regional transport systems work surprisingly well, the bevy of involved health professionals may occasionally discuss among themselves and dispute details and management of a case without all of the relevant facts being available to them. And, they then sometimes share those opinions with distraught parents, or via the chart with an inquisitive attorney, again without review of the record itself.

On other occasions the fetal monitoring equipment either does not work, is applied in a faulty manner, or may not be available.

Each of the above cases (modified slightly from actual occurrences) exemplifies various types of recurring problems. With appropriate thought and planning, each might have been avoided, or the risks of suffering and human loss reduced, in addition to the financial losses which resulted. In June 1982, the American Medical Association adopted a position paper on electronic fetal monitoring that would warrant review by each physician and each hospital involved with obstetrics. The summary recommends that "continuous fetal monitoring is clearly warranted in high risk pregnancies . . . moreover, it is clear that many intrapartum events may occur which might change a low risk pregnancy to a high risk one.

"If fetal heart rate monitoring is performed: (a) it should be done at least every 30 minutes during the first stage of labor; (b) it should be done at least every 15 minutes during the second stage; (c) in both situations it should be performed for a period of 30 seconds after the uterine contractions.

"The use of electronic fetal monitoring in low risk pregnancies should not be denied the patient, or her physician, if requested."

What You Can Do

Is there an effective peer review process in your hospital's obstetrical unit? Does it involve the nursing services? And is patient opinion sought about the quality of your service as seen through the patient's eyes?

In your hospital, is increasing attention being given to delivery room/ delivery suite activity? Even more importantly, are the medically appropriate things being done so that they can be documented? Just who is accountable for reviewing the adequacy of the records, and for enforcing corrections of deficits? Are there appropriate arrangements to deal with the issue of electronic fetal monitoring? Again, who is accountable and responsible for appropriate implementation?

Remember, avoiding one $200,000 "bad baby" case could result in a premium saving of approximately $50 for each of the more than 4,000 insured physicians in Washington.

More important than the economic impact on physicians, implementation of appropriate measures in your hospital will result in higher quality medical care for your patients.

SECTION 15

Wrongful Birth, Wrongful Life

Case.   D. H., a 29-year-old para 0 gravida 1, was diagnosed during her fifth month of pregnancy as having idiopathic epilepsy. She was treated with diphenylhydantoin ("Dilantin") for control of her seizures and delivered a normal term infant four months later. Post partum, the Dilantin was continued. One year later, D. H. sought the professional opinion of three different physicians about any possible risks involved in her having additional children while being maintained on Dilantin. Each of the three doctors responded that Dilantin could cause cleft palate, hirsutism, and other possible abnormalities. None of the doctors conducted literature searches or consulted other sources for specific information regarding the correlation between Dilantin and birth defects.

Discussion

Relying on the assurance given her, D. H. carried two subsequent pregnancies to term, with both of the female offspring subsequently being diagnosed as afflicted with the "fetal hydantoin syndrome." Mr. and Ms. H. subsequently brought suit against the three physicians—all of whom were in the military—alleging that because of their negligence (their failure to uncover appropriate information and provide appropriate advice), the H's had suffered a "wrongful birth." In other words, were it not for the faulty advice, neither birth would have occurred, and because of the births, the H's had, in fact, experienced financial damages.

The Federal District Court then sought the opinion of the Washington State Supreme Court on the questions of law involved, and the court, accepting the facts of the case as transmitted to it, recently ruled on the issues involved. Because of the implications of that ruling, and the predictable speculations which are bound to follow, it is relevant here to review the State Supreme Court's action.

The Justices grasped the significance of their task of attempting to extrapolate legal principles and practices derived from our English heritage into the modern world as it has expanded under the impact of science and technology. In years gone by, physicians were unable to predict with any validity the likelihood of birth defects; today, in many instances, we can. In years gone by, relatively "failsafe" contraceptives and abortion techniques were either unknown or unavailable; today, they are both known and available. A century ago, "defective" children usually succumbed after delivery; today, many survive. Fifty years ago, our medical information storage and retrieval system was primitive—it usually existed in the head of the expert; today, it's been converted to print media and computers and is able to respond at the touch of a keyboard.

These changes and others permit the question to be posed: In accepting a patient contemplating pregnancy, does the physician have a duty to advise the patient according to each of these points? The court concluded that such a "duty" does exist. The court also concluded, on the basis of the facts brought to it, that the involved physicians had breached that duty.

Next, the court wrestled with the question of the parents' rights to act on such information. What can parents do if informed that a significant risk of a defective child occurs? While the court remained silent on the issue of using contraception (apparently accepting it as a fact of twentieth-century life and not subject to current dispute), it spoke out quite forcefully as to its conclusion. The court concluded that, upon hearing of significant risks for a defective child, the parent(s) does(do) have the right to terminate that pregnancy.

And, finally the court recognizes that the added burdens and costs of caring for a defective child, as opposed to a normal child, should be treatable as damages, subject to recovery from whatever parties failed in their "duty" to inform the prospective parents so they could exercise their right to avoid defective birth should they so choose. The outcome of such failure would be termed a "wrongful birth." In their opinion, the State Supreme Court went one step further to consider the offspring's position and potential rights and concluded that he or she, too, ought to be justified in seeking financial recovery for any extraordinary expenses incurred in reaching the age of majority, i.e., to cope with the rest of a "wrongful life."

To reiterate, the State Supreme Court recognized the "duty of the physician" in today's world to advise in full when queried about possible birth defects. On the basis of the facts of the case cited, it concluded that the duty had been breached and that the bad outcome caused damages, which, in turn, should be subject to recovery.

As is apparent, many extrapolations from this position are obvious. Attesting to this is the publicity given to its implications for the abortion question. Opponents of abortion cite the court as siding with the parents as opposed to the fetus in sustaining the prerogatives of the parents. There has been considerable speculation about the extent and range of the duty of the "prudent physician" to advise the patient contemplating pregnancy. How the physician will be able to respond is not clear. Where, for example, is the physician to turn to update his or her knowledge or potential risks with relative certainty; will he or she be subject to "reverse risk," i.e., overcaution in providing advice so that someday "wrongful nonbirth" might be an issue? In fact, there is precedent for such speculation based on an early 1980 Washington case. There the parents had sought amniocentesis; the physician concluded that the risks outweighed the benefits and chose not to perform one. When the child was found to be defective, suit was successfully brought against him. Had he performed the amniocentesis and had a subsequent loss of the fetus occurred, would the physician have been subject to an allegation of "wrongful nonbirth?"

Suffice it to conclude that mechanisms for updating information are essential; quick, accurate, complete, and reliable storage and retrieval services (i.e., library services) would seem to be mandatory.

At a time when, paradoxically, the federal government is seriously considering modifying its current rules which require a hospital to maintain a medical library to participate in Medicare/Medicaid, the incongruity is awesome. Meantime, the AMA is well on the way to working out with General Telephone an opportunity to bring modern information storage and retrieval systems to the individual physician's office. WSMA has been involved in discussions and support of library services in the past, but its leadership has chosen to let its participation lapse. One of its committees is wrestling with that matter at the present time, trying to encourage the development of a good state-wide system, but with a paucity of funding. Fortunately, multiple county medical societies have taken the bull by the horns and are formulating good information storage and retrieval systems.

Supporting the contention that there is a need for such a system are the following facts. The case under discussion had its origins in 1971–72; the D.H.'s afflicted infants were born in 1974 and 1975. In my opinion the "fetal hydantoin syndrome" was not well described until 1975, and was not widely recognized and accepted by the profession until sometime thereafter. Prior to that time, it was known that epileptic patients on anticonvulsants did have an excess in birth defects, but professional opinion was divided (and such division is well recorded) as to whether it was the epilepsy or the medication that was responsible. These data were carried to the jury which heard the case brought against the manufacturer in the state court and that jury found for the defendant. But the trial judge, Judge Tanner, hearing the military physicians' case in the U.S. District (Federal) Court, found for the plaintiff and prompted the Supreme Court's consideration. It is possible that an appeal through the federal court system now underway will see a reversal based on the facts, but a reversal would not alter the subsequent recognition of "wrongful birth" and "wrongful life" issues. Other state courts have already acted in this area. Common sense can't help but support the contention that a clear duty does exist for the physician involved; the extent of that duty remains ill defined.

What You Can Do

In your community, where would you turn to conduct a literature search, such as is called for in the case report? Do you have access to such a service? Do you know how to use it? Do your colleagues use it? Does your medical staff ever check to find out if the called-for searches have, in fact, ever been carried out?

Washington is fortunate in having an effective library network system involving hospitals, medical societies, and the University of Washington; we have a toll-free telephone consultation MEDCON program to the medical school, a statewide poison information network, and a drug information network—all of which are aimed at helping the physician fulfill his or her duty. Do you use and support these programs?

SECTION 16
Managing Malformed Infants

Case 1. J. D., a newborn male, was discovered shortly after delivery to be affected with esophageal atresia with associated tracheo-esophageal fistula plus Trisomy 21 (Down's Syndrome). His parents and physician adopted a position of no surgical intervention. Over the subsequent six days, his case was discussed across the nation with significant medical, legal, and ethical debate. The issue was temporarily resolved when the Indiana courts supported the parents' decision, holding that they (the parents) did, in fact and under those circumstances, have the right to decline therapeutic remedies.

Shortly thereafter, a somewhat comparable case occurred in a neighboring state, but in that situation the court took the opposite position and instructed that surgery be undertaken. During both cases, considerable friction occurred among the involved health professionals as they took sides—broadly painted as either in favor of or opposed to maintaining life for children. Sometime later in the spring, the Department of Health and Human Services activated "Baby Doe squads" to investigate and rectify situations wherein newborns were purportedly being denied appropriate care in hospitals across the country. Predictably, these led to still further polarizations of professional feelings and considerable public discussion and distrust about what was going on.

Case 2. F. M., a newborn female, was the second child born to an Rh-negative and previously sensitized Jehovah's Witness who had declined Rh-immune globulin because it was a blood product. The cord Coombs was positive, and the four-hour bilirubin level approached 7 mg percent. The child was transferred to a tertiary care center; plans were initiated to undertake exchange transfusion. When the parents declined to give consent on religious grounds, the juvenile court was consulted. It, in turn, arranged "guardianship" and cleared the way to accomplish the transfusion immediately. Follow-up proved uneventful, and the child was discharged home on the fifth day of life. Interestingly, during the entire process—at least as far as could be determined—the medical and hospital staff all seemed to accept without debate the appropriateness of the court's intervention. No one but the paternal grandparents took issue with involving the courts, including, interestingly, the parents. In fact, in contrast to the prior case, court involvement was applauded as the way to go.

Case 3.   T. B., a 36-hour-old male, was transferred to a medical center for management of an imperforate anus. The product of a normal pregnancy of, and an uneventful vaginal delivery by, his 39-year-old mother, T. B. had been recognized as having the clinical features of Trisomy 21 (Down's Syndrome) shortly after delivery— flattened occiput, characteristic appearance to the eyes, slightly full and protruding tongue, a simian crease on both hands and feet, and diffuse hypotonia, plus a loud heart murmur on ausculation and extreme cardiomegaly on chest x-ray.

Physical examination of the rectal area at the time of transfer demonstrated a thin veil of almost transparent tissue covering the rectal orifice. Surgical relief of the rectal problem was felt to be relatively simple to achieve, but the cardiac signs and symptoms were interpreted as indicative of a major cardiac defect likely to cause death in the absence of attempts at surgical relief.

At that point in time, the parents were presented with the perceived facts and the options available to them. They considered the alternatives overnight and then decided against surgical intervention. Then the involved attending physician, who had been ostensibly neutral, shifted and supported their position, as did the consultant surgeon. Other members of the medical staff disagreed totally with the decision against intervention. The nursing staff emphasized their "Catch 22" quandary: if they fed the child and he eventually aspirated, it could be considered as active euthanasia; if they withheld all fluids, it could be construed as intentional starvation, also an active euthanasia process. Much private one-on-one discussion and debate followed, but virtually no group discussion and/or meetings intervened. At the end of 48 hours, the child was transferred to a nursing home for terminal care. Some 10 years later, members of the staff who participated in the process continue to harbor unease about that situation and the mechanism of its management.

Discussion

While none of the above cases depicts a traditional malpractice situation with the associated financial price tag, each overflows with the potential for controversy. During the ensuing days, weeks, months, and, in one case, a decade, hard feelings have been evident among the health professionals involved in these trying situations. Very basic philosophic differences exist among them regarding the issues; obviously, there are no simple solutions.

Four letters to the editor in the December 15, 1983 issue of the *New England Journal of Medicine* decry the position of the Indiana court which sided with the parents. A fifth in the January 5, 1984 issue chides the American Academy of Pediatrics for not exerting pressure and using all resources to salvage any and all handicapped infants. On the other side of the issue is Strong's telling article in the September 1983 *Law, Medicine, and Health Care*, citing study after study of the dire consequences to family stability as they try to cope with handicapped children. The point of concern is, of course, that the misery and antagonism embodied in such situations not be permitted to interfere with the already stressful environment of the hospital (and all its inherent potential for error) to precipitate inappropriate allegations of malpractice. Studies from industry document repeatedly that, under such stressful circumstances, the likelihood for error increases enormously; excessive stress stretches the tolerance of the system beyond its capacity, and errors inevitably follow.

What can be done to avoid this type of problem? First and foremost (and an unachievable ideal) is to avoid the situation precipitating the stress. Unfortunately, the 1980s hardly seem the time for the reduction of stress in our hospitals. When the issue of terminating life-support systems for the "hopelessly" ill individual is compounded by that of possibly withholding definitive treatment of malformed infants, and these philosophic conflicts are added to the consideration of "Diagnostically Related Groups" and health care quality, stress upon the system is obvious. If avoiding stress is impossible, the next best measure is to anticipate that such problems can and will occur and then act accordingly.

Responsible committees and leaders of the medical staff will want to take time to get the issue on their respective agendas to encourage discussion and debate (and probably ventilation) from their constituencies. These, in turn, should be followed by the development of a critical path of management. Resulting policies and the best judgment of individual physicians permit practices to reflect "reasonable and prudent professional" consideration of the issues. Assured telephone availability of staff leaders to participate in or moderate management programs of critical patient care problems is essential. Nighttime and/or weekend voids are simply not acceptable.

Devoting medical staff meeting time to discussions of the issues at hand is highly desirable, even if controversy follows. Again, quoting from an article in the December 15, 1983 issue of the *New England Journal of Medicine,* "Indeed a survey of the attitude of a hundred young trainees in family practice revealed that 86 had a positive attitude toward alternative medicine. Of these, 21 had referred patients for treatment and 12 had made referral to nonmedically qualified practitioners—a step which only a few years ago would have led to disciplinary action by the General Medical Council (the body responsible for control of the medical profession in Britain)." Obviously, change is underway and consideration ought to be given to involving other health professionals in such discussions in the future—nurses, aides, pharmacists, therapists, and hospital administrators. In essence, open discussion as a means of reaching solutions, as opposed to restricted-access, smoke-filled-room arrangements, seems the best agenda for the future.

With regard to the Baby Doe decision, the Reagan Administration is of the opinion that the federal government needs to be involved in assuring that the rights of the infant will be protected. By and large, the profession has championed local problem solving as the way to go, emphasizing the use of "Infant Bioethical Review Committees." Agreeing that the responsibility is awesome for the individual empowered to appoint the committee and that, no doubt, the courts will be asked to become involved throughout, currently this route seems the most attractive alternative (or, perhaps, the least unattractive). Agreeing in advance that the decisions of such committees can't help but be imperfect, the process would seem, nevertheless, to exemplify our best effort for now.

What You Can Do

In your hospital, are you aware of what, if any, procedures are to be followed in "no code situations," in terminating life support, in withholding care for malformed infants? How does a new medical staff member discover the existence of such steps? Has anyone ever checked on the validity of the oft-heard "everybody knows that. . . ." Does anyone review records to assure that the procedures are actually followed?

As noted above, it must be possible to manage malformed infants in such a way as to avoid those situations which are guaranteed to lead to disputes and allegations of malpractice. Do your part to avoid such occurrences.

7

Drug Issues

Drug prescription and usage, an issue hardly affecting the malpractice scene a generation ago, is today a growing cause of suits, accounting for as many as 20 percent of the claims in Washington State. The statistics themselves can be overwhelming; more than 90 percent of the therapeutic nostrums employed pre-mid-twentieth century have now disappeared from the U.S. Pharmacopeia and have been replaced by natural or synthetic chemical entities with enormous potential for good, as well as for harm.

Since 1965, more than six million new chemical entities (not all of them drugs) have been identified. Many are being investigated for their pharmaceutical (i.e., "controlled toxic") effects as individual items and in combination or in given individuals with unique genetic make-ups. What with the average hospitalized adult receiving an average of 13 different drugs on multiple occasions (for children the number is 7), the opportunity both for the unexpected and for error is enormous. And, if the truth be known, this source of trouble has the potential for taking over the lead—especially as modern technology permits the pinpointing of cause. By itself this issue is able to resurrect therapeutic nihilism as a way of life for practicing physicians.

Section 17. Complications from Drug Usage
Section 18. Errors in the Usage of Drugs
Section 19. More Drug-Related Problems
Section 20. Drugs Indicted, But Not Convicted

SECTION 17

Complications from Drug Use

Case 1. H. S., a $2^1/_2$-year-old female, was seen in an emergency room with a 12-hour history of apathy, anorexia, fever, and vomiting. Sepsis was suspected and the child was admitted for diagnostic procedures and appropriate treatment. Blood, CSF, and urine were obtained for culture; CBC and urinalysis proved compatible with a septic process.

Within an hour the patient was begun on a course of penicillin and Gentamicin; no electrolytes, BUN, or creatinine were obtained. Over the next 72 hours, her symptoms appeared to resolve slowly; all cultures remained sterile. Antibiotics were discontinued on day 8; subsequently she demonstrated signs and symptoms of aminoglycoside toxicity. Conduction deafness, confirmed by audiometry, proved to be persistent; vestibular impairment over a six-month period appeared to be less of a problem. Approximately $1^1/_2$ years after the episode, a negligence action was brought against the physician, the hospital, and the manufacturer of the antibiotic on the grounds that the deafness had been totally preventable. A significant award followed.

Case 2. R. B., a 28-year-old female, consulted her physician for a perceived weight problem. In addition to other approaches, the physician prescribed an amphetamine derivative, and the patient obtained prescription renewals on numerous occasions over the ensuing years despite the lack of objective evidence of obesity (she weighed less than 115 lbs). Eventually the patient brought a negligence action against the physician claiming his therapy was responsible for her addiction to amphetamines. She received a significant award.

Case 3. W. W., a 38-year-old woman, had been using birth control pills for almost six years; without warning she had a stroke resulting in a partial permanent neurologic disability. She brought a negligence action against the prescribing physician alleging malpractice because she had not been properly informed of the risk. Her suit was successful.

Discussion

Each of the aforementioned cases involves an alleged error in the prescription or use of a drug. Fault was found for three quite different reasons. In the first case, it was claimed that the physician failed to test the patient for her ability to handle the drug's metabolism and thereby avoid toxic consequences. In the second, the claim was made that the physician had used the drug for "non-therapeutic purposes." In the third case, the argument was that the physician had failed to obtain an informed consent from the patient before prescribing the drug (i.e., that the patient had not been made aware of the risks).

Different preventive measures and precautions are called for in each of these instances. Furthermore, additional problems can arise with the use of drugs which call for still different precautionary techniques. The point, however, is that drugs and their use or misuse account for a sizeable number of malpractice claims and awards. According to the 1980 report of the National Association of Insurance Commissioners, injuries attributed to drugs were distributed as follows: 19 percent due to anesthetic agents; 13 percent due to hormones; 12 percent due to antibiotics; and 8 percent due to analgesics. Among the 1,003 anesthetic agent incidents, the average indemnity was $96,822.

A recently completed claims study in Washington State showed that 20 percent of open claims are related to drugs, with most attributable either to improper administration or inappropriate prescription. The reserves for these cases alone amount to more than $2 million—some 20 percent of total reserves.

Confirming the presence of problems is the recently completed Washington State Professional Standard Review Organization audit on the use of aminoglycosides. The audit showed that a third of the patients receiving those drugs for more than five days apparently failed to have either a BUN or creatinine measured prior to, or early in, the course of therapy. This is in clear opposition to standard recommendations. The PSRO's studies have also confirmed that while RhoGAM (Rh-immune globulin) is being used extensively in term deliveries—almost without fail—it is being omitted in as many as 30 percent of pregnancy terminations. Remember, such omissions can cause clinical harm and justified litigation—even many years later.

What You Can Do

Do you always review the potential risks of a drug in your own mind and, if severe, also with the patient prior to prescribing? If preliminary lab tests are called for do you obtain them, and follow through to review the results? Can someone claim that you prescribed tranquilizers, barbiturates, or opium derivatives for inadequate indications? At your hospital, does your Pharmacy and Therapeutics Committee monitor adverse drug reactions or establish programs to eliminate possible drug interactions?

Malpractice claims and awards related to drugs can be predicted to rise as new and more effective drugs enter the marketplace. They are not going to disappear. Ask yourself how these new drugs might expose you and your patients to risks, and act accordingly.

SECTION 18

Errors in the Usage of Drugs

Case 1. T. S., a 14-month-old male who had always been well, developed diarrhea and fever. Examined in an emergency room, he was admitted to the hospital for rehydration. Serum electrolytes were within normal limits; an IV of normal saline was begun, and after approximately 100 ml, he voided. At that time an order to add 30 mEq of K (potassium) per liter of administered fluid was apparently misinterpreted; instead 30 mEq was added to the IV reservoir, with the result that it ran at a concentration of nearly 60 mEq of administered fluid, which would amount to a concentration of 600 mEq per liter! As would be expected, shortly thereafter T. S. developed relentless bradycardia, hypotension, and cardiopulmonary arrest; permanent damage occurred. In the end both the physician and the hospital (nurse) were held culpable for the way the order was written, as well as how it had been carried out.

Case 2.   W. K., a 34-year-old male, attempted suicide with salicylate, as well as several different sedatives plus alcohol. On arrival in an emergency room he was unconscious; respirations were only minimally increased; pH of the blood was 7.41 and urine pH was 5.5. To enhance urinary excretion of the salicylate, orders were written for 2 mEq per kg of body weight of sodium bicarbonate ($NaHCO_3$) to be added to the IV of 1,000 ml of 1/4 percent normal saline. Somehow a mistake occurred and instead of adding $NaHCO_3$, KCL was given, with the predictable results. Somehow, moreover, it had been added directly to the reservoir rather than to the bag of fluid.

Case 3.   G. D., a 59-year-old female, was admitted to an ICU for management of a suspected coronary occlusion. On the second day it was decided to further dilute some heparin that was to be added to her IV of 5 percent glucose. The dilutent, which for some unknown reason was also used to rinse out the system, was to have been 0.9 percent (normal saline). Somehow that vial got mixed up with three other vials that were on the bedside table—one of which was KCL. The result was that G.D. received at least 18–20 ml (36–40 mEq) of KCL solution before the error was recognized. In her case, fortunately, there were no dire consequences.

Case 4.   T. H., an 11-month-old female, was brought to Seattle to receive treatment for acute monocytic leukemia. During that program, allegedly she was to have received 15 mg of potassium over some four hours, but instead had it administered over a 10-minute interval (at least according to the local newspaper report). Again, the result was cardiopulmonary arrest which, when recognized and treated, had already progressed to irretrievability.

Case 5.   J. W., a 65-year-old male covered by Medicare, had a long history of angina and congestive heart failure; the latter was treated initially with salt restriction and digitalis. After some 10 years of relative stability, J. W. was given a diuretic and supplemental KCl (potassium chloride). Problems ensued and, despite manipulations of the diuretic dosage, J. W. pleaded with his physician to discontinue the diuretic. The physician agreed. Unfortunately, J. W. failed to discontinue the KCl supplement, and his physician failed to notice the omission. Several months later, potassium-related symptoms appeared and J. W. was admitted to hospital with a serum potassium of 7.1. He threatened a suit but, fortunately, declined to follow through.

Discussion

Each of the above cases illustrates a problem with the use of potassium and the writing and implementation of orders related to that use. Pharmacologically, we've come a long way since the mid-1950s when the IV use of potassium really began. Initially it was limited to the management of prolonged diarrhea, but today it is used as a replenishment for adults using certain diuretics. In controlling cardiac functions during heart procedures it proves to be life-saving. Some physicians, however, use it for a remedy of almost anything that ails a patient. It is in "elective situations" where potassium's use is overly abundant. If errors were able to be eliminated from everyday life there would be no serious consequences, but such errors do happen and these cases illustrate that Murphy's Law seems to be constantly in action in our hospitals. Before the introduction of the unit-dose system in pharmacies in the mid-1960s, three studies were done in teaching hospitals focusing on the frequency of drug errors.

Error is involved in as many as one in every six drug administrations. Fortunately, most such errors were related to the timing of the administration but a number of other errors, such as wrong drug, wrong dosage, occurred. Since the average adult on the average medicine service got some 13 to 16 different drugs (with most on multiple occasions), it is little wonder that anyone gets in and out of hospital without a significant drug problem. Perhaps things are better today, but have you seen any data actually gathered to substantiate the increased safety of the unit-dose system?

I have mentioned earlier the problem of illegibility of orders, of the ease of mixing up similar-appearing as well as similar-sounding drugs (and of the necessity to avoid verbal orders), as well as the dangers inherent in the use of abbreviations; a myriad of things can go wrong. Just recently, in the Seattle area, a 44-year-old diabetic patient on dialysis reached for some castor oil to relieve her constipation in the middle of the night. Mistakenly she took instead a bottle of "oil of wintergreen"—100 percent methyl salicylate. After she had drunk a considerable amount, she then went on to further mis-identify the bottle to the physician as Ben-Gay lotion. By the time all the errors had been straightened out, the patient had begun to have convulsions and shortly succumbed to a cardiopulmonary arrest.

Drug-related problems used to account for less than 5 percent of malpractice claims; at last count they played the leading role in more than 19 percent of claims, and many of those (particularly those related to anesthesia) were associated with large pleas and large awards.

In the 1920s, when $HgCl_2$ (mercuric chloride) was used as a diuretic, the tablet was shaped in the form of a coffin and the container had "POISON" imprinted on the glass itself. Today, drugs are no less potent; while all prescription drugs used in the state of Washington and 80 percent of over-the-counter drugs used here have some form of imprint identification, the opportunity to double-check the accuracy of the drug and its dosage is rarely taken advantage of. Conceivably, episodic monitoring of patient prescription usage would heighten sensitivities of physicians as well as patients to this significant hazard. Used appropriately, drugs are effective; used erroneously by physicians, patients, or intermediaries, they can lead to disasters and predictable claims of liability.

What You Can Do

In your office, have you developed a system to double-check on your use of drugs—patient profiles, office stocks, prescription handouts, etc.? How is the system implemented, and who is responsible to see that it is?

In your hospital, has there been a problem with IV potassium, with oral potassium, with drugs in general? Is your Pharmacy and Therapeutics Committee reviewing patient profiles for accidents in administration? Does anything happen as a result? Moreover, do those involved physicians, nurses, and pharmacists get together to pinpoint these problems and develop appropriate solutions?

Currently WSMA and the Washington State Pharmaceutical Association have a joint program underway to better inform patients of drugs and their benefits. It's timely, indeed, for physicians to be as certain as possible about the appropriateness of the drugs and dosages being used.

SECTION 19

More Drug-Related Problems

Case 1.   M. J., a 37-year-old woman, had been under continuous psychiatric care for some eight years. Her depressive condition had been complicated on several occasions by psychotic episodes. While she was hospitalized for one episode, phenothiazines were prescribed and continued at a reduced level following discharge. She was still taking the medication two years later when she developed tremors, involuntary head and neck movements, and was found to have "drug induced tardive dyskinesia." Subsequently, her husband brought a malpractice action claiming negligence on the part of the prescribing as well as the attending physician, and he threatened to sue the manufacturer. After prolonged investigation, discussion, and debate, a modest settlement was made.

Case 2.   E. T., a 26-year-old woman, visited her physician because of signs and symptoms of urinary tract infection; pus cells were seen and a culture obtained. Ampicillin capsules were prescribed. Somehow a mix-up occurred at the pharmacy: the patient was given Dilantin capsules instead. She took several capsules and in less than 24 hours developed lethargy, dizziness, and ringing in the ears. She returned to her physician who examined the capsules and immediately discovered the source of the problem. Over the next 24 hours the symptoms cleared, but the patient felt long-lasting sensations of light-headedness and impaired concentration. She threatened a liability action, and after considerable (and no doubt expensive) explorations, a suitable settlement was agreed upon.

Case 3.   N. D., a 2,200-gram premature male infant, was suspected of having sepsis or meningitis and was put on antibiotics, including an aminoglycoside. Cerebrospinal fluid proved to be normal but a blood culture grew a coliform organism. Antibiotics were administered for 14 days, but no drug levels were obtained. (Actually, at that time, except for research drugs, the drug levels were not obtainable.) As the child reached his first birthday, it became increasingly clear that he was deaf. Shortly thereafter, an action was initiated alleging that the aminoglycoside was responsible and that it was, in fact, prescribed in excessive dosage and for too long, and moreover, was really not needed in the first place. Despite widely divergent expert testimony, the plaintiffs eventually prevailed.

Case 4. T. C., a 35-year-old woman, had recurrent urinary tract infections. She had received several sulfa drugs, nitrofuradantin, and finally chloramphenicol. Shortly after completing a two-week course of the last drug, she developed petechiae and was found to be anemic. She was diagnosed to have "drug induced aplastic anemia." Allegations directed at the manufacturer were shortly dismissed because that complication had been so well publicized in so many ways, including the package insert. However, allegations directed at the physician were not so easily managed because two controversial points were raised. Was the potential "cost/benefit" brought to the attention of the patient and her informed consent sought? Was the potential complication itself ever shared with the patient? While the answers to these questions remained clouded in doubt, the patient fortunately did recover physically. She also recovered a sizeable monetary award.

Discussion

While the appropriate use of new drugs has curtailed disease and comforted patients, inappropriate use is fraught with problems for patients, for physicians, and for insurance carriers. Even their appropriate use can occasionally cause problems. An analysis of the 711 claims closed in Washington between 1975 and 1980 and of those still open in 1981 reinforces the point: drug-related claims continue to increase. They went from being the basis of less than 5 percent of all claims prior to 1970, to 10 percent of those closed by 1980, to almost 20 percent of those still open. A study conducted by the National Association of Insurance Commissioners in the late 1970s confirms that drug-related claims are an increasing cause of malpractice actions.

The problems are multiple: failure to choose an appropriate drug or an adequate dosage; failure to monitor for side effects; failure to initiate proper monitoring; and simple technical errors with decimal points, abbreviations, legibility, and verbal orders.

A recent book, *Medication Errors: Causes and Prevention*, by Davis and Cohen (1981) serves to remind us that such errors were even more prevalent in the 1950s and 1960s before "unit dose systems" were widely employed in hospitals, before drug dispensing in hospitals was placed in large part in the pharmacy, before the Joint Commission and professional groups began to clamp down on verbal orders. In addition, since that time, drug imprint practices and laws have come into being, permitting rapid and accurate tablet/capsule identification via the coded information on the tablet or capsule itself.

The problem of keeping the patient informed about drug-associated risks deserves to be stressed; a $1 million-plus settlement connected with a contraceptive agent serves as an example. Physicians need to exert greater effort in discussing such issues with patients and in advance of problems. Perhaps helpful in deciding where to begin is the National Association of Insurance Commissioners' report that anesthetic agents, hormones, antibiotics, and analgesics are the predominant causes of liability actions, with settlements in excess of $95,000 for each anesthetic case involved. In the field of drugs, abiding by the "standard of carefulness" is critical and applicable to all physicians regardless of specialty.

What You Can Do

In your hospital is there an active effort to discourage verbal orders. Is that effort supported by the physicians themselves? Does your staff encourage or discourage multiple physicians writing orders on a single patient? If so, who—if anyone—monitors for drug interaction problems? What happens if a drug error is detected? Does your Pharmacy and Therapeutic Committee review all such problems to seek corrective measures?

In your office, what kind of record do you keep to support your contention that you do appropriately instruct patients in the use of drugs?

SECTION 20

Drugs Indicted, But Not Convicted

Case 1.   D. B., a 27-year-old mother of one, had experienced considerable morning sickness with her first pregnancy. Pregnant for a second time, she sought relief and her obstetrician prescribed Bendectin, a chemical compound in use for some 25 years by more than 30 million patients and repeatedly appraised for possible side effects with negative findings. At term, D. B. delivered an infant with congenital defects of the extremities; subsequently, she brought a liability action against the physician involved and the manufacturer. The jury found for the defendant physician on the one hand, but, although it exonerated the drug of any causal relationship to the deformities, it nonetheless awarded a sizeable amount to the plaintiff from the manufacturer's carrier.

Case 2.   On Thanksgiving morning, J. S., a 10-month-old female, was seen "gumming" several leaves of an amaryllis plant. Seeking advice from the local poison control center, J. S.'s mother was instructed to induce vomiting using Syrup of Ipecac. This she did with satisfactory results. Later that afternoon, she called the poison center again because J. S. had vomited on two more occasions. She was instructed to administer clear fluids. The next morning she called again because vomiting had recurred, and after affirming that she had, in fact, used the syrup rather than the fluid extract form, she was again reassured but advised to contact her private physician for further direction. This she did. He sought out the details of the situation and, suspecting complicating "flu," reiterated the clear fluid routine. Nothing more was heard until the next morning (Saturday) when she again called because vomiting had persisted, although urine output was apparently still normal. At that point, she arranged to visit her physician, who was a family medicine resident. J. S. was examined and found to be active, hydrated, and not apparently significantly ill. By coincidence, several senior "attending physician supervisors" were present that Saturday morning in the clinic and they, too, took a quick look at the child, agreeing with the decision for more clear fluids, a phenothiazine suppository, and home observation with frequent telephone follow-up. At approximately 11:30 that morning, the mother called back to her physician saying that J. S. seemed satisfactory, had voided again, and appeared to be holding down small amounts of clear fluid. But, at 12:30, she called again, hysterical: J. S. had suddenly stopped breathing. Only two blocks from the hospital, J. S. was taken there immediately and, after 40 minutes of attempts at resuscitation, was declared dead.

During the resuscitation efforts, an attempt at intracardiac epinephrine administration saw peculiar greenish-black fluid aspirated via the syringe. A "stat" x-ray revealed an air-filled mass in the left chest, which, at post-mortem, was found to be an infarcted herniated stomach and portion of the duodenum. Speculation held that repeated vomiting had led to the herniation or that a congenital diaphragmatic defect was exacerbated by the emesis, permitting the herniation to occur.

Subsequently, an action was brought against the physician and his program, claiming negligence. Laboratory tests determined a serum sodium in excess of 180 mEq, said by some experts to be diagnostic of "hypernatremia." Coexistent with that elevated serum sodium was a normal serum chloride and a serum bicarbonate of approximately 50 mEq—all from a blood sample taken during the agonal phase just *after* a large bolus of sodium bicarbonate had been administered. After considerable analysis and review, a settlement was made.

Case 3.   S. V., a 35-year-old woman, was seen for repetitive kidney infections by her physician; he recommended an IVP. Arrangements were completed, and before the procedure she was advised by the radiologist that administration of the contrast material might cause, among other consequences, unconsciousness. Fortunately, that particular reaction did not occur but, unfortunately, the patient developed phlebitis in response to the dye administration, with subsequent complications.

She brought suit, claiming negligence on the part of the radiologist for not having mentioned phlebitis as a risk of the procedure during the obtaining of her "informed consent." In late June 1983, the Washington State Supreme Court upheld a lower court's dismissal of her suit, holding that a medical risk does not have to be mentioned unless it is "significant and likely" and that expert testimony must be presented to substantiate such a position. This ruling would appear to reinforce the "reasonable patient–prudent physician" posture of informed consent and argue against the claims of some that physicians must present any and all possible consequences in seeking an informed consent.

Discussion

Each of these three cases provides a glimpse at a different element of the professional liability scene as it relates to drugs. The first case, involving Bendectin, is only one of more than 30 such cases which are currently being resolved. It has led the manufacturer to withdraw the drug from the market, despite current strong scientific evidence and governmental recommendations as to the absence of any association between Bendectin and the purported defects. For today's practitioner, however, the message is a clear one. When the popular press views a chemical with enough alarm—be it Bendectin, or aspirin as it is tied to Reye's Syndrome, or dioxin (Agent Orange) as it is blamed for a number of syndromes—one would be wise to avoid using the controversial chemical unless no alternative exists and then only if the patient agrees to the possible risks in writing. As a purist, one can fault such a posture; as a pragmatist, one had best act on the basis of discretion. The better part of valor under these circumstances would be to avoid the conflict, but to encourage political policymakers on the one hand, and the world of science on the other, to persist in seeking out the truth of the matter. A look at the future suggests this type of issue will be a burgeoning cause of conflict.

The second case is of particular concern to the author. More than two million cases of accidental poisonings have been managed with Syrup of Ipecac, with no undue consequences of this variety ever having been seen. When confronted by the uncertainty of this type of case, is it still warranted to advise induction of emesis, especially when the yield is admittedly so low, i.e., 10–30 percent of unabsorbed ingestant? Having no other evidence of toxicity, such approach seems reasonable; one "reaction" in two million would seem not enough to redress the balance of benefit. Washington State's poison centers are continuing to advise induction of emesis as a policy when unknown as well as known toxicities lurk at the other end of the phone.

Of equal concern here is the evidence presented that during the adjudicative process several experts seemingly spoke inadvisedly in holding the physician negligent for not recognizing "hypernatremia" when quite obviously it occurred only at the time of death and consequent to the administration of a bolus of sodium bicarbonate. For the reader the point is that drugs long accepted as safe may not always be so, and the practitioner has to be very wary and on guard for possible problems with old acquaintances.

In contrast to the first two cases, which can't help but heighten physicians' anxieties, the third should be reassuring, appearing to support a common-sense approach to the informed consent issue. It reiterates that the patient has a right to be involved in the decision-making process touching on his or her life and that the physician must be prudent in providing appropriate information to help the patient in his or her decision-making. As Melvin Belli mentions in his concluding article in *Medical Economics* (June 23, 1983), the issue of informed consent continues to be in flux as it undergoes "conceptual evolution." It will no doubt play a larger role for all of us in the future. Washington State's Supreme Court appears to have adopted the "reasonable court" position, providing a reassuring complement to the "reasonable patient-prudent physician" philosophy.

What You Can Do

In your practice, have you reviewed your drug usage habits to insure that you have excluded any controversial problems? Do you avoid aspirin for children with flu and/or varicella? Do you avoid methaqualone as possibly having abusive potentials far outweighing any remote therapeutic benefit? Where do you stand on chloramphenicol? Phenylbutazone? Percodan? Alcohol?

In your hospital, does your Pharmacy and Therapeutics Committee review the use of "risky drugs" and not simply argue about formulary inclusions of antibiotic profiles? If not, why not? Do you have access in your hospital's pharmacy or emergency room to the AMA's 1983 publication "Drug Evaluations"? And, are communication lines open to assure that you can get accurate advice when local drug information proves insufficient?

8

Documentation Difficulties

When the solo practitioner was a G.P. who made house calls and dispensed innocuous medicine, there was little use for an extensive medical record. Usually no other health professional was involved; lab tests were few and medicines simple. That is not the case today; the medical record is, rightly or wrongly, the coordinative vehicle for diagnosis and management, for hospitalized patients in particular. Estimates are made that on a given day as many as 20 different health care professionals may initiate an action directed at a patient based on information gleaned from the patient's chart. No longer is that chart simply a mechanism to jog the physician's memory. Today's patient's record contains historical information, laboratory information, and fiscal information, all thought to be critical to the delivery of quality medical care. And each record is in itself a threat to the confidentiality of the patient's private matters, which further complicates the issue of record management. Even with the computer to help, all is far from well in this "crossroad of medical care traffic."

91

SECTION 21

Delays in Reporting Untoward Incidents

Case 1. S. T., a 62-year-old male, was admitted to hospital for coronary artery by-pass surgery in 1978. Preoperative work-up was entirely as expected; both the patient and his family were informed about the potential benefits, as well as the risks, of the procedure. During the procedure a technical problem developed in the pump oxygenator "temporarily" impairing oxygenation. To the best of the recollections of those present, it was recognized "quickly." Postoperatively, only a cursory note was entered into the chart. The patient was slow in regaining consciousness and subsequently evidenced significant CNS impairment compatible with that associated with hypoxemia.

Approximately 24 months later a negligence action was brought against both the physician and the hospital. Interestingly, neither the carrier for the physician nor that for the hospital had been informed of any potential problem; no incident report had ever been initiated. There was much difficulty in developing an appropriate defense, in large part because personnel had moved, records were "too succinct," and the equipment had long since been dismantled and replaced. The decision for a large settlement ensued.

Case 2. G. T., a 28-year-old para 1 gravida 2, was admitted to the hospital in labor. Taken to the delivery suite, she was found to be at term with no prenatal problems and with contractions every four minutes. Labor progressed satisfactorily; after two hours the fetal heart rate was noted to have slowed to 82 beats per minute. With the cervix fully dilated, the attending obstetrician quickly ruptured the membranes; the amniotic fluid was meconium-colored. Delivery was completed rapidly and the umbilical cord was found to be looped twice around the infant's neck. APGARs were depressed; the infant was slow to breathe and remained "depressed" for several days prior to going home. Over the next nine months his development was definitely slowed. When the child was approximately one year of age, a negligence action was initiated against both the physician and the hospital alleging failure to monitor labor adequately. Neither the physician's nor the hospital's carrier had received any indication of the existence of a possible problem. Again, *no incident report* had been prepared for either the physician's or the hospital's carrier.

Discussion

In both the above cases, the involved physicians failed to notify their insurance carriers of the existence of a possible problem. In the former case, the delay apparently contributed to a significant award. In the latter case, despite the delay involved, but with much additional time and expense, the defense counsel was able to establish an effective defense. The jury decided in favor of the physician and the hospital. The essential lesson: Any delay in reporting a suspected problem only compounds the difficulty of mounting an appropriate defense.

Based on a careful review of Washington's claim experience, some 41 large claims averaging $230,000 each (for a total of almost $9.5 million) have been identified in Seattle. An average of more than 24 months elapsed between each of the 41 precipitating events and the reporting of them to the carrier by the physician involved. Only nine cases were reported in the first six months after the events occurred.

To help avoid these delays, the WSMA prepared and distributed a simple "incident report" form to use in the office or the hospital to alert the carrier to possible or potential malpractice problems. Many hospitals and carriers have done likewise. The details of the form are inconsequential; its prompt transmittal is the critical issue. Submitting such reports can only help expedite dispute resolution; current carriers and WSMA have adopted a policy that submitting the reports, per se, will affect neither an individual's premiums nor his or her insurability. The physician should keep blank forms in easily accessible sites and use them appropriately or telephone the carrier's representative to make a verbal incident report. The earlier the report, the better the defense attorney's and carrier's ability to formulate a successful defense, or to arrange an individual settlement. As a general rule, such reports are intended to remain confidential communications between the physician and the carrier and the carrier's attorney.

What You Can Do

In your hospital are incident report forms actually used? If so, for what purposes? Is the medical staff involved in submissions, or in resolving the causative problems? Does the Executive Committee of the medical staff ever review the issue?

If you were the chief of service at your hospital, how would you try to avoid delays in reporting? As an attending staff member, what can you do to avoid such reporting delays in the future?

Errors can never be totally avoided. When you begin to look for them you will find them far more common than you had ever dreamed. A reduction of 10 percent in their frequency is still a reduction. Insist that this aspect of quality assurance gets high priority.

SECTION 22

Failure to Transmit Lab Results

Case 1.   At noon on a Friday, W. M., a primipara, delivered an entirely normal infant after an uncomplicated pregnancy and labor. Prior to delivery she had been tested as Rh negative with negative titres, a prime candidate to receive Rh-immune globulin (RhoGAM) if the baby were to test Rh positive, which he did. Whatever the cause— failure to transmit that result promptly to the chart, cross-coverage by her obstetrician's associate, forgetfulness, the occurrence of a long holiday weekend with reduced nursing staff—no Rh-immune globulin was ordered. Furthermore, the "fail safe" check system failed to catch the omission. The patient was well into her next pregnancy when the prior sensitization was detected. A negligence action was initiated, citing not only the effect on the second infant—transient hyperbilirubinemia—but also the parents' mental anguish in contemplating future pregnancies. An award was made.

Case 2.   T. F., an eight-year-old male, fell from his bike, injuring his right elbow on a Sunday afternoon. Seen by his family physician in an emergency room, his arm was not casted after an x-ray revealed "no fracture." A radiologist reviewed the x-ray the next day and interpreted it as revealing a fracture through the epiphysical plate. The radiologist's amended report was sent to the emergency room via "routine" channels, with the result that it was filed in the ER record, but was not transmitted to the family physician. Six months later, problems in recovery had become evident. The communication failure was recognized and a negligence action was brought successfully against the radiologist and upheld on appeal.

Case 3. M. T. was born after an uncomplicated pregnancy via an entirely normal vertix delivery, his mother's third child. Routine care was given; a PKU and thyroid screen were drawn and were dispatched to the lab. A positive PKU test was reported back to the hospital, and dutifully filed in the medical record without notifying the attending physician. (The system has now been corrected!) Since the baby's problem was not known, no dietary restrictions were even considered. Subsequent developmental delay led to a repeat PKU test at 10 months of age. The positive result tripped detection of the previous positive test and climaxed in a very sizeable financial settlement.

Case 4. N. N., a 42-year-old married woman with long-standing surgically confirmed fibrocystic disease, felt a new lump in her right breast. Biopsy confirmed a well-differentiated encapsulated carcinoma. In view of the patient's refusal to submit to radical surgery, extensive tumor board discussion led to a recommendation of "lumpectomy," plus careful follow-up with repeat biopsy of any new mass for consideration of radiation therapy. Over the next several years, three repeat biopsies were performed following the detection of new lumps. The first two were negative, but the third was interpreted as positive. At that point the patient agreed to radiation therapy, which was begun. Midway through therapy an amended report, reinterpreting the most recent biopsy as negative, was made to the operating surgeon, the family physician, and the radiation oncologist. The last, believing strongly that radiation had been indicated initially, completed the course of therapy without mentioning the amended report to the patient. Apparently the other involved physicians assumed the radiation oncologist would discuss the situation with the patient. According to the patient, however, he made no such mention of an amended report, nor did her other two physicians. She did suffer minor complications from radiation.

Later the patient moved to a distant community. There her new physician requested and received a copy of her records. He was startled, to say the least, that the patient denied any awareness of the amended negative biopsy report. She subsequently brought a negligence action based on a lack of an informed consent. "Of course I wouldn't have proceeded if I'd known the biopsy was negative rather than positive—after all it's up to me to choose." A settlement followed.

Discussion

As more and more lab tests, x-rays, and consultations are performed, the chance of error goes up exponentially. Miller and colleagues demonstrated more than two decades ago how infrequently a positive finding of glucose on a routine hospital admission urine actually tripped demonstrable action on the part of the attending physician. That problem was corrected only by physically covering up all positive entries on the chart with orange fluorescent tape, apparently appealing to the voyeur in all of us. Miller's group hypothesized that information overload was, in fact, the underlying cause of inaction. Information overload shows no signs of decreasing, so the problem continues today at all levels of practice and in all types of hospitals.

Several years ago at Children's Orthopedic Hospital in Seattle, a JCAH-WSPSRO mandated audit revealed that 28 of 30 newborns (who had been transferred there because of severe acute medical or surgical problems which proved remediable) had been discharged home without called-for PKU testing. Not surprisingly, the "management system" was modified immediately; subsequently five random re-audits have detected not a single omission. The innovation activated in response to the problem actually worked.

In 1980, with the cooperation of Washington's hospitals, an area-wide audit was conducted on the use of Rh-immune globulin. For term and premature deliveries, the track record was remarkably good. Among the some 6,000 potential recipients, all but three had been tested and treated appropriately.

But, for patients undergoing termination of pregnancy at a time when Rh sensitization is a risk, less than 75 percent had appropriate diagnostic or screening tests performed and/or Rh-immune globulin given.

At another hospital in Washington, three unrelated simultaneous hospitalized patients had the same last name, and the same first two initials. Only an alert nurse saved a transfusion error from occurring when she confirmed both her patient's name as well as his unit number before starting his blood transfusion.

In summary, failure to transmit a significant laboratory value or x-ray interpretation appropriately constitutes a dereliction of duty. Failure to notice (i.e., receive) the result or not to look for it is equally negligent. Thus, the interpreting cardiologist must act when he or she notes an acute myocardial infarction in a routine preoperative EKG. And the operating surgeon is equally responsible to carefully review "routine" lab tests before proceeding, particularly when the outcome of a test may increase the risk of a procedure.

What You Can Do

In your hospital, have you as an individual, or has your Medical Executive Committee, taken the initiative to assure that lab medicine, pathology, and radiology communications are prompt, clear, concise, and immediately recognizable if abnormal? Do physicians work with, or simply gripe at, pathologists and radiologists who are trying to keep up with information dissemination techniques? Who is making sure that everyone is not simply trying, but also succeeding? Finally, who really pays attention to illegible handwriting or confusing abbreviations? Let's hope it is not simply the plaintiffs' lawyers.

SECTION 23

Altered Records: Non-Defensible

Case 1. C. A., a 29-year-old multipara, consulted her lawyer alleging faulty quality care during her most recent delivery. Her attorney obtained a copy of the hospital record and, after outside obstetrical consultation, filed suit. During the pretrial investigation, the attorney obtained a second copy of the hospital record and found it to contain much defense material that had not been present in the original record. The additions and modifications of the record forced an early settlement of an otherwise defensible case.

Case 2.   M. D., a 40-year-old male, was seen in a physician's office for eye symptoms and was allegedly provided with a thorough examination. At a subsequent date, however, he developed glaucoma and claimed malpractice. An initial review of the examining physician's office records was reported to reveal no tonometry testing; however, a second copy of the record differed from the first copy in that additional material supporting the defense had been entered into the chart. Once again, the purported alterations eliminated the possibility of any successful defense.

Case 3.   An elderly patient, M. S., and his attorney brought suit claiming negligent treatment of a cutaneous malignancy because of the development of an ulcerating lesion attributed to radiation therapy. A review of the treating physician's records raised questions about the timing and source of the entries there; a handwriting expert testified that all entries were made with the same pen, with the same ink, by the same person, and probably on the same date. Here, again, the perception of an altered record was a critical element in losing the case.

Discussion

Each of the above instances is presented to emphasize the disastrous consequences of altering records or appearing to have altered records. According to an analysis of claims closed in Washington over the past several years, there are three to five cases terminated each year in favor of the plaintiff after altered records have been detected and exposed.

What ought to be done if additional information warrants being entered into the chart or if a correction is clearly called for? First and foremost, avoid any suggestion of deception. Legal experts recommend striking a single line through the erroneous material and then inserting the correction or addition so it will be clearly identified, and, finally, dating and signing (legibly) the entry. If a copy of the record has already been obtained by the plaintiff one ought to consult his or her defense attorney about any options available. Under no circumstances try to deceive anyone; it simply won't work.

What You Can Do

Do you always provide adequate documentation after meeting with a patient? Do you ever insert additions after the fact without identifying them appropriately? Do your office colleagues follow such a course of action? At your hospital, do your medical staff colleagues always refrain from inappropriate alterations of records? If you answer yes, how can you be sure?

Simple additions to the record appropriately dated can be a valuable asset in providing continuing care; in contrast, after-the-fact insertions purposely camouflaged can destroy any defense against a malpractice action.

9

Standard of Care

In most states, a physician's care is expected to measure up to "standards." But often standards are nebulous or not relevant, or even non-existent. How, for example, can the soon-to-retire senior physician possibly pursue the same standards of technical care as last year's chief resident, or how can that resident measure up to the senior physician's professional maturity in his "standard of carefulness." Regardless, expectations are high for both parties. And expectations are also high for the medical staffs and hospitals who appoint such individuals to practice on their premises. Harking back to yesteryear when the "locality rule" was dominant has no place in modern medicine. Telephone, radio, television, and the print media make available to the community physician, regardless of location, access to the latest detail of the artificial heart on the same day it is being implanted. At the same time, all of us need to realize that the "standard of care" traditionally has more often been interpreted as "what is" than "what should be."

SECTION 24

The Public's Expectations of Competency

Case 1. M. S., a 23-year-old previously healthy male, developed increasing abdominal pain accompanied by nausea and vomiting. Admitted to a community hospital by his family physician, he was seen in consultation by a general surgeon, who concurred with the diagnosis of suspected appendicitis and advised continued observation and appropriate hydration. Over the next 12 hours, localizing physical signs developed; systemic toxicity progressed and an appendectomy was scheduled. At operation, perforation was apparent and considerable purulent peritoneal fluid was noted. Appendectomy was completed, drainage established, and antibiotics instituted.

Over the next three days, however, the patient's condition progressively deteriorated. His fever increased, he experienced notable upper abdominal tenderness, and he developed a cough. Possible right pleural fluid was detected on a chest x-ray. A second abdominal exploration was undertaken and more drainage instituted. Several attempts of thoracentesis produced no return, and on the seventh postoperative day, M. S. was transferred to a Seattle tertiary-care hospital for further treatment. Surgical drainage was rearranged, more "appropriate" antibiotics were substituted, a subphrenic abscess was evacuated, and hyperalimentation was begun.

Some 48 days later, M. S. was discharged in a debilitated but stable condition. Subsequently, a malpractice action was instituted, alleging negligence in the details of initial case management, particularly with reference to the postoperative course and the delay in arranging transfer to the tertiary-care hospital. A Claims Review Panel and its Professional Review Committee both concluded probable negligence for much of the postoperative period.

Case 2. P. V., a 26-year-old female (para 2 gravida 4 abortus 1), sought routine prenatal care through a birthing center arrangement involving a sponsoring physician and a licensed midwife. During the last trimester, her blood pressure rose (the diastolic reached 92 mm/Hg on one occasion) and protein was found in the urine. Other than salt restriction, no specific treatment was instituted. When labor began, P. V. was brought to the birthing center. Contractions increased appropriately and labor seemed to progress satisfactorily—save for the detection of still more protein in the urine and a diastolic pressure recorded repeatedly to be above 90. Suddenly, P. V. had a seizure. Standard management for toxemia was employed; the infant was delivered rapidly and both mother and infant were transferred to a hospital.

When the child was examined at approximately two years of age, moderate neurological impairment was detected; it was ascribed to perinatal events. A liability action was instituted, holding the physician-midwife duo to have been negligent in not making a diagnosis of toxemia sooner or arranging for more expeditious transfer of the mother to the hospital. The Claims Review Panel reviewed the case, recommending settlement.

Case 3. W. D., a 54-year-old male, consulted his regular family physician about a group of "hyperkeratotic" pigmented skin lesions over his back, which had apparently increased in size during the prior six months. In actuality, he had other similar lesions on his forehead and elsewhere on his body. The physician proceeded to excise several of the lesions, but submitted none of the specimens for tissue review. Approximately six months later, with the onset of systemic symptoms and weight loss, the patient was re-examined and the diagnosis of metastatic melanoma was established. Shortly thereafter, a suit was instituted.

The Claims Review Panel heard the details of the case, including the defendant physician's position that, "I've always managed cases this way over the past 25 years," and "There was no convenient way for me to arrange appropriate microscopic review." Needless to say, settlement was encouraged and corrective measures about practice patterns were instituted.

Case 4. S. H., a 38-year-old morbidly obese male, had sought many opinions about possible remedies. Finally, he agreed to undergo an intestinal by-pass procedure to be performed by a board-qualified general surgeon in a relatively small community hospital. There followed a series of anesthetic, cardiac, and surgical complications. The operating surgeon and the family physician attempted to cope locally, but finally transferred S. H. to a larger community hospital in a nearby city. A long and stormy course of recovery ensued; as expected a malpractice case was instituted. When presented to the Claims Review Panel, and in light of prior incidents involving the same problem with the same surgeon, a strong recommendation for settlement followed.

Case 5. M. N., a 26-year-old female, sought out cosmetic surgery for her nose. She consulted a plastic surgeon, and arrangements were made to carry out the necessary procedures in his office. Unfortunately, the patient experienced an untoward reaction to the anesthetic agent, necessitating cardiorespiratory resuscitation. The necessary resuscitative equipment was not available in the office, and M. N. died. This tragic death resulted in a large settlement for negligence.

Discussion

Probably more than ever before, individual physicians and surgeons providing patients with either medical or surgical services and hospitals providing the necessary supporting services are being expected to meet standards of "quality assurance." The community takes it for granted that the physician will be capable and competent—trained and experienced—in what he or she intends to do or in arranging for a patients' transfer elsewhere for appropriate care.

The public also expects hospitals to have skilled personnel and technical equipment available to deliver what patients need, or to have established liaisons to get the services delivered elsewhere. In essence, the public expects medical care not only to appear to be a system, but actually to be one. What 50 years ago was a cottage industry of individual entrepreneurs with a far more limited concept of public accountability has undergone enormous transition and change in its public image and in the public's expectations. Moreover, the perceived change outstrips the real one. And the consequences are obvious.

Each of the foregoing cases illustrates a failure to keep pace with the public's expectations. Certainly, the involved patients made a voluntary choice in the first two cases; when a problem occurred, however, prompt remedial action appeared not to have been undertaken. The third case illustrates the failure to maintain practice patterns congruent with current expectations; and the fourth saw delinquent behavior, which was actually a *pattern* of behavior, prove critical. Case 5 clearly demonstrates the importance of having adequate equipment in physicians' offices, as well as in hospitals.

As a more general observation, many medical staffs are failing to keep up with expectations about the credentialing process on the one hand, or the profiling of physicians' and surgeons' hospital activities on the other. For example, in 1982 a Washington physician moved from one city to another and sought new staff privileges. The new hospital promptly collected and validated by letter his credentials, carefully considered his qualifications, and granted him the requested privileges. Only after a problem arose and some telephone calls were made did it become apparent that the medical staff's credentialing process had failed to detect the fact that three other hospitals had decided against renewing that physician's staff privileges. Perhaps the major fault lay with the recommending hospitals. A case in point involves several Boston physicians who strongly supported a physician's application to a Buffalo hospital for staff privileges, but neglected to note that he had already been convicted of one rape charge and was awaiting action on two others.

The message is clear: as medicine's services have improved, the public's and the profession's expectations have increased exponentially. Physicians individually and collectively must keep pace with new expectations.

What You Can Do

In your hospital, does your Surgical Service and Tissue Committee carefully review the types of surgical cases by individual surgeon? Do they actually serve as the physician's "keeper"?

Does your Pharmacy and Therapeutics Committee assist your pharmacist in reviewing the prescribing patterns of individual staff physicians, with particular attention to the use of drugs with significant side reactions or drug interactions? Has your Quality Assurance Committee created a mechanism to review the management of complications of surgical cases which prolong hospitalization past the 75 percentile? And, finally, does your Credentials Committee use telephone inquiries as well as written documents to validate an applicant's credentials?

None of the above is easy or inexpensive; however, failure to perform such activities proves even more difficult and far more expensive.

Maintaining "Standards of Carefulness"

Case 1. S. H., a 17-year-old male always in good health, developed mid-abdominal pain after track practice. Over the next two hours, it became more severe, assumed a peri-umbilical location and was accompanied by mild nausea. Four hours after the onset of pain, S. H. went to his physician. He felt somewhat better, had no point tenderness (it remained "diffuse"), had a normal rectal exam, and reported less nausea.

By ten o'clock that evening, however, S. H.'s pain had worsened, localizing in the right lower quadrant, and nausea had increased dramatically. Shortly after 11 P.M., he began to vomit, his fever rose to 102°, and the localized pain suddenly disappeared. He called his physician who offered reassurance and ordered ice chips and clear fluids by mouth. Vomiting continued and increased throughout the night. By 6:30 A.M. his temperature was over 103° and he was in acute distress. He was transported to the hospital and shortly thereafter underwent appendectomy with the findings of a ruptured appendix; postoperative drainage and eight days of hospitalization followed, with apparent recovery. A suit against the physician claiming failure to diagnose and failure to abide by the standard of care was instituted and eventually settled.

Case 2. D. C., a seven-pound, two-ounce newborn male, born of a 24-year-old sensitized Rh negative para 2 gravida 5, had been diagnosed as afflicted with hemolytic disease of the newborn by prenatal amniocentesis. Within an hour of delivery, confirmatory tests had been completed and an exchange transfusion begun. During that procedure, which was "routine" at the time, it was decided to add calcium gluconate to the system. The circulating nurse obtained the medication, scrubbed the top of the vial, and held it as the pediatrician aspirated two ml into a syringe and injected it slowly into the system. As the last drop disappeared from the syringe, the nurse cried out "Stop! That's sodium sulfadiazine!"

The exchange process was continued. Neither pulse nor blood pressure changed; the urine remained free of problems and the child's course continued otherwise uneventfully. Even so, thereafter, that pediatrician has always personally read the label on each and every vial of medication he has administered. Just recently, however, one of his colleagues did not do so, and inadvertently substituted intrathecal methotrexate with ominous results.

Case 3. T. Y., a 76-year-old woman, fell at home about 10 A.M. and developed acute hip pain. She was transported to a nearby emergency room by automobile. Seen first by an ER physician and then by her own physician, she was felt to have a possible hip fracture and was sent for x-ray; otherwise she was fine. She returned to the emergency room about noon to await the interpretation of the films. After about an hour, a nurse approached saying her physician had called from his office to say that she could go home because there was no fracture. She was taken to the car in a wheelchair, driven home and carried into the house, complaining of acute pain. A follow-up call to her physician brought instructions to return to the ER; a review of the films demonstrated a clear diagnosis of fracture, and an uncomplicated pinning and repair followed.

Although no lawsuit was filed, considerable embarrassment and dismay was felt and expressed by both of the involved physicians, each of whom believed that the other had agreed to review the films and call if a problem was found. Neither, it turned out, had either seen the films or contacted x-ray about them; hearing nothing, the family physician had ordered discharge. Steps were instituted by the ER to avoid such a mishap in the future.

Case 4. C. G., a 54-year-old severely myopic woman, complained of blurring and gaps of vision, and had a borderline elevated tonometry reading. Direct ophthalmoscopic exam without pupillary dilation proved normal; visual field exam was not carried out. Over the next two years, C. G. was seen on numerous occasions without further tests. Glaucoma was then diagnosed with a severe associated visual loss. A negligence action was brought and developed along two lines: first, that the patient was not informed that additional diagnostic steps were available; and second, that the care rendered did not measure up to Washington's "standard of care." The State Supreme Court upheld the plaintiff's point of view and an award followed.

Discussion

Each of these cases has elements in it to be judged against medicine's "standard of care." Richard S. L. Roddis, University of Washington law professor and a longtime consultant to WSMA, recently provided a detailed analysis of current "Washington law as to the applicable standard for determination of negligence in medical malpractice cases." He emphasizes that it is "any conduct (including nonaction) which deviates from an assumed normative standard of carefulness," stressing that the term "carefulness" more closely denotes the "reasonably prudent person standard" than does the word "care," which often is interpreted to reflect only the current accepted professional practice standard.

Professor Roddis stresses the courts' insistence that juries be given maximum leeway in deciding what is or is not "reasonably prudent behavior." Because of the technical nature of medicine, however, both courts and juries have tended to look toward current practice of the profession as the standard reflecting reasonably prudent behavior, because neither court nor jury has the expertise to make an independent judgment.

Nonetheless, three recent Washington Supreme Court decisions have reiterated the "prudent physician standard," as opposed to the community practice, with two going so far as to say that failure to test for glaucoma (regardless of age) is in itself, as a matter of law, sufficient evidence of negligence to award a plaintiff verdict, regardless of the community's customary practice.

This point warrants emphasis. In the past many physicians have been under the impression that the "locality rule" limited their exposure to the extent that, insofar as they abided by the customary practice of their community, they would avoid a plaintiff verdict. Even when the locality rule was abolished and supplemented by the "in the State of Washington" phrase, most physicians continued to look at the professional standard of behavior as the test. Not so, said the Washington Supreme Court loudly and clearly. It is the standard of carefulness of the reasonably prudent health provider as judged by the jury which supervenes. On occasion, the issue of imprudence has seemed very clear in the court's mind. For example, under *Helling v. Carey*, the Supreme Court has declared the necessity of conducting a procedure so obvious that failure to do so has been determined as a "matter of law" to constitute negligence.

In summary Professor Roddis emphasizes four important points:

1. "The prevailing customary practice among other physicians is not the conclusive standard for the determination of negligence in medical professional liability cases in Washington. The prevailing standard of practice continues to be an important test and probably governs the results in most cases. However, when a plaintiff can produce other evidence indicating that the defendant physician's conduct was imprudent, it is open to the jury to find liability, irrespective of the standard of practice. The shift in emphasis toward a reasonably prudent physician standard affects both the tenor and thrust of the evidence developed in trial and the climate of settlement."

2. "It is particularly interesting that all three of the Supreme Court cases involved diagnostic failures. The liability door has opened wide, both in Washington and in other states in the diagnosis area, particularly because of the double-push of expansive application of the informed consent doctrine and erosion of the controlling effect of prevailing factors as the test of negligence."

3. "One would hope that the appellate courts will not pursue the propensity for deciding that various medical procedures are required 'as a matter of law' other than in certain highly unusual cases. Otherwise, we will find ourselves with a judicially-authored manual on required defensive medical practice."

4. "I doubt that a further effort to legislatively re-establish a conclusive standard of practice test for medical negligence would succeed."

What You Can Do

In your hospital, does any mechanism exist for your medical staff to consider whether a given diagnostic or therapeutic measure employed by one of its staff physicians meets the current standard of carefulness?

Is your medical staff actively working with one another and with other members of the hospital staff—particularly with nurses and pharmacists—to develop a system of checks and balances to protect the patient on the one hand, and each other on the other, from claims of ignoring the standard of carefulness?

Does your medical staff tolerate a physician who inappropriately deprecates or criticizes a nurse for behavior he or she believes is in the patient's best interest?

While many would seek a return to the good old days of the community's professional practice as reflecting the standard of care, that apparently is not about to occur. Do your utmost to see how your patients can best be served by you as a "reasonably prudent physician." It will not only be in your patient's best interests, but also in yours and all other practitioners'.

SECTION 26

Reiterating Standards of Care

Case 1. The plaintiff, B. H., had an intermittent history of recurrent iritis. As a consequence of yet another bout, she visited an ophthalmologist, Dr. A. After examination, he confirmed the diagnosis and prescribed topical as well as systemic steroids plus atropine eyedrops. He checked her eyes weekly for approximately one month, as a remission seemed to occur. Approximately two months after her last visit, B. H. began seeing a flashing light and wavy lines; within weeks she experienced a sensation of ocular pressure, particularly in the right eye. She returned to Dr. A. and was re-examined. He increased the dosage of the steroids but the symptoms persisted. She then returned and was seen by Dr. B., who made a diagnosis of acute glaucoma. Emergency eye surgery followed. While the immediate postoperative period was uneventful, B. H. did have several subsequent brief hospitalizations and her vision continued to deteriorate significantly. Over that period of time, she also developed some psychological problems, and shortly thereafter filed a malpractice action, directed at Dr. A. and the pharmacist.

Discussion

Argued in a lower court, the finding for the defendant physician was eventually appealed to and heard by the Washington State Supreme Court. Their decision was released in the spring of 1983; that opinion addressed several important points bearing on the malpractice scene and on risk management programs.

1. First and foremost, the court found, as a matter of law, for the plaintiff in her allegation that the dispensing pharmacist had, in fact, given her isopto-carpine, which constricts the pupil, instead of the prescribed atropine, which dilates it. While the full details of the precise cause of the error were not immediately available, the point to be emphasized is that the possibillity of a dispensing error is lurking in every pharmacy, just as the chance of a prescribing error exists in each prescription written. Many experts hold that an irreducible error rate exists. Since the likelihood of error is an exponential function of the number of actions taken, keeping the number of drugs prescribed to a minimum is essential in an effective risk management strategy.

2. Regarding B. H.'s challenge to Dr. A., the court found that her allegation was ill-founded and, on the basis of the defense presented, rejected it. In developing the opinion, however, its author, Justice Robert Utter, emphasized and reiterated several important points about the "standard of care" in Washington. He recalled that during the legislative action of 1976 and in light of the legislative intent to clarify the issue of the standard of care, some subtle and some obvious changes had been introduced. The concept of the "prudent practitioner" standard had been emphasized as a replacement for the "customary practice" standard heretofore used. While the wise physician will continue to consider both in his or her daily practice, he or she ought to recognize Justice Utter's reminder that the state medical association's legislative effort to avoid permitting the court to exert its standard had not succeeded. (Utter cited the court's ruling in *Helling v. Carey* (1973), in opposition to expert testimony, that tonometry ought to have been used in a patient 30 years old with possible glaucoma [Curran and Shapiro 1982]).

On several subsequent occasions the State Supreme Court has reaffirmed that the prudent physician behavior standard is to be *the* standard and that the definition of "prudent physician behavior" remains the prerogative of the court and not simply of the profession. Here, too, the inference ought to be clear to all in dealing with risk management efforts: the standard of care that physicians practice must be in agreement with the prudent physician's practice as opposed to the usual community standard if the likelihood of fault is to be minimized.

3. At the same time, Judge Utter teased out a single word from the 1976 legislative action and zeroed in on it, as it set precedent. The WSMA had urged that the standard of care would, in fact, be established in part related to learning practiced by the professional. During the bill's passage through the legislature the word "practiced" was transferred to "possessed by." As a corollary, when plaintiff B. H. introduced a nonphysician (a physiologist) to testify as an expert, the Supreme Court ruled that the lower court had *not* erred in accepting that testimony, but had acted correctly when it subsequently chose to disqualify the physiologist for unrelated reasons. The point for emphasis is that a non-physician is able to be seen by the courts as an expert and is likely to be called upon in the future.

In the past, physicians and their organizations have been criticized for their apparent reluctance to review, critically analyze, and speak out on some of the purportedly questionable testimony provided by both plaintiff and defense experts. In *Pediatrics,* November 1982, Brent wrote eloquently on the topic; at the interim meeting of the AMA House of Delegates in December 1983, an official report noted that some experts are receiving $3,000–$5,000 a day to serve as experts, and that hence the possibility exists that on occasion exaggerations take place. Yet critical review of such testimony has not materialized. If testimony is found misleading, the errant expert physician need not necessarily be disciplined—simply publicizing his words ought to suffice to inform his peers so that they can reassess their judgment of his professional competence.

Addressing the issue of legislative activity in the November 3, 1983 issue of the *NEJM,* Curran (well-known Boston professor of legal medicine) highlighted the Rand Corporation's study on the impact of the 1975 legislative enactments across the nation as they were directed to solve the malpractice crisis. While some alteration in frequency of claims subsequently took place, changes in severity apparently did not. He notes that "in the states where a financial limitation was placed on awards and in those where the collateral source rule was repealed or modified, the severity but not the frequency of awards was reduced substantially. *No other substantive legal reform*—and there were many across the country—*was found to have any* statistical relation to reduction in either the frequency or severity of claims. Most surprising, perhaps, is the fact that the establishment of screening panels to eliminate spurious or nonmeritorious claims seems to have had no comparable effect in reducing the total number of claims. Also, the limitations imposed on contingency fees for plaintiffs' lawyers were not found to affect either the frequency or the severity of claims."

Perhaps proposed tort reform elements being introduced into the 1984 legislature will be more successful, but risk management efforts, including careful review of expert testimony by bringing to light erroneous statements, ought to prove even more helpful. One can be certain that both physicians and non-physicians will continue to be called upon to testify; can we be equally certain that that testimony will have peer review in the future?

What You Can Do

In your hospital, does the medical staff or the Pharmacy and Therapeutics Committee review drug administration, with the possibility in mind of reducing the total drugs given and, in turn, reducing error?

In your practice, have you reviewed your actions against the "prudent physician behavior" standard as opposed to the "community standard"? Both ought to be followed—but currently the former cannot be overlooked. And, finally, are you formally discussing with your colleagues what the role of the expert witness should be?

SECTION 27

Coping with Medical Advances

Case 1. W. C., a 26-year-old female, delivered a stillborn 2,960-gram male infant after a normal pregnancy and labor. Preliminary post-morten examination revealed multiple areas of intestinal obstruction, which were believed to be the consequences of congenital malformation. This interpretation was conveyed to the mother without any elaboration.

Approximately 14 months later, W. C. delivered a live-born female infant, who shortly thereafter developed evidence of an intra-abdominal problem. She was quickly transferred to a tertiary-care center, where intestinal obstruction was diagnosed and a final diagnosis of cystic fibrosis established and reported to the parents. After considerable counseling, the parents sought an explanation as to why the diagnosis had not been considered or established in their first infant. Subsequently, and to the chagrin of many, it was discovered that the microscopic components of the original autopsy had never been completed; when it eventually was done, the diagnosis of cystic fibrosis was apparent. One possible explanation for the oversight is that the hospital's quality control mechanism relied on each patient's having a hospital unit number assigned to him/her. The original stillborn infant—being stillborn—unfortunately never received such a unit number and, as a consequence—the fail-safe monitoring system failed.

Case 2.   T. D., a 32-year-old pregnant woman, together with her husband, inquired of her obstetrician about the possibility of Down's Syndrome occurring in her fetus. The couple was obviously disturbed by that possibility and highly desirous of an amniocentesis to exclude it. In line with the community practice at the time, the obstetrician discouraged amniocentesis, and T. D. went to term where, after an uneventful labor, she delivered a female infant with Down's Syndrome, including its heart-anomaly component. Subsequently, the D.'s brought suit against the physician under the concept of "wrongful birth." The physician was responsible for impeding the prenatal diagnosis and thus the choice of terminating the pregnancy, which, not being terminated, resulted in the birth of a malformed infant for whom he was responsible. As has happened in other states, the lower court approved a large award.

Case 3.   D. H., a 30-year-old male, consulted Dr. T., a board-certified orthopedist, because of recurrent pain in and about his neck. He had already undergone medical treatment and traction therapy with very little relief from symptoms. After an appropriate history and physical examination, Dr. T. recommended a neck operation to "relieve the pressure and eliminate the problem." The patient agreed to the surgery. Postoperatively, not only did D. H.'s symptoms continue, but also he developed clear evidence of a new neurologic defect in his lower extremities.

D. H. brought suit against Dr. T., alleging negligence; his attorney sought the expert opinion of several other local orthopedists who were quite vocal in their condemnation of Dr. T. Dr. T.'s defense attorney sought and secured supporting expert testimony from a distinguished professor in a nearby academic institution, supporting his client's competency. Eventually, however, the hospital's medical staff was brought into the dispute, along with the state's professional society, the medical association, and the Medical Disciplinary Board. The final results were that a libel suit brought by Dr. T. against the orthopedists was settled, Dr. T's carrier paid a considerable sum to the patient, Dr. T.'s license was suspended, and he left the state. In retrospect, it is clear that Dr. T.'s performance was short of ideal, but of equal importance was the deficit in the performance of the entire medical staff involved. It turned out that the specific procedure that Dr. T. had used on this patient occurred with greater frequency in his community (which housed but a single hospital) than in the entire city of Chicago.

Discussion

Each of the above cases serves to emphasize the perhaps all-too-obvious point that advances in medical practice now available in the 1980s bring with them a concomitant increase in exposure to allegations of negligence. Increased ability to diagnose hereditary disease and counsel factually on the implications of such findings imposes new and significant obligations on the profession.

In the first case, the combination of circumstances led to a failure of appropriate completion of a routine post-mortem examination. Had it been completed and the presence of cystic fibrosis reported to the parents, the second pregnancy would probably have been avoided. The standard of care is quite clear in this particular situation.

In the second case, the physician had actually followed the professional recommendations regarding amniocentesis that were prevalent at the time. But he might be said to have been less than sensitive to the parents' concerns. Conceivably, a second opinion might have strengthened his position on the one hand, or might have clarified the intensity of the parents' feelings on the other, to such an extent that his recommendation might have been altered.

In the third case, one could and would take issue with the actions of the practitioner, as well as of the "corporate" medical staff at the hospital where he operated. Had that medical staff been looking at the surgical procedures being done in terms of the individuals involved, they would certainly have noted the astronomical frequency of this relatively unusual procedure. In similar fashion, had the medical staff in a California hospital kept tabs on what was happening within its institution, they would have uncovered the infamous Dr. Nork prior to his being involved in liability actions costing in excess of $12 million. Enter Risk Management programs!

In early November 1982, representatives of the Washington State Medical Association's Risk Management Program and Washington's Physicians Insurance Company attended a meeting in Dallas, Texas, to share experiences about Risk Management programs. The meeting brought together representatives of the then 29 physician self-insurance companies. For each company, the goal was the same: to assist their insureds in avoiding allegations of negligence.

The program in Washington consisted of Claims Review panels, a Professional Review Committee, closed-claims analysis and data analysis, and "Case of the Month" presentations in "WSMA Reports," with Risk Management Review Units being used on the local scene. This program was particularly well received, and WSMA plans to continue and expand each element in the future. The program in Oregon was also highly acclaimed, particularly their entertaining and informative television tapes depicting vignettes of malpractice and how to avoid the same situations. These taped programs are now being used throughout Washington, too, in hospitals, at medical societies, and at specialty society meetings. WSMA is also contemplating (1) publishing a quarterly bulletin along the lines of one in Arizona, (2) possibly borrowing a correspondence course developed in Pennsylvania, and (3) emulating audio cassettes developed originally in Oklahoma and Missouri—all aimed at complementing its efforts at improving the insurance component of the malpractice scene on the one hand, and its efforts at tort reform on the other. All physicians are encouraged to get involved in their hospitals' quality assurance program or in their medical societies' related grievance hearings.

What You Can Do

In your hospital, is there a visible quality control program monitoring the delivery of laboratory, x-ray, and EKG reports to the phy-

sician and to the chart? When was the last time you heard about how
the program was doing?

Does your surgical service have available data to review the distribution of case loads by individual surgeons? Does your Pharmacy
and Therapeutics Committee have a way of looking at the prescription practices of the medical staff, with regard to antibiotics and tranquilizers, sedatives and steroids?

The concept of medical staff corporate responsibility is here, but
the staff cannot fulfill its obligations without an adequate information base. Some hospitals have subscribed to Michigan's Professional
Activity Survey program; others have developed their own "management information programs." Only a few actually dissect, analyze,
interpret, and act on the data collected. Is yours one?

SECTION 28

Standards for M.D. Availability

Case 1.   K. S., a 26-year-old married woman, was admitted to a
military hospital on Independence Day, 1979, in labor. Progress was
alleged to be satisfactory and fetal monitoring was carried out. Suddenly significant fetal bradycardia ensued, followed by purported
cessation (or absence) of heartbeat for two to three minutes, during
which time reportedly no remedial intervention was undertaken. The
outcome: a damaged infant.

In a decision rendered in February 1983, the U.S. District Court
awarded $11.7 million consequent to perceived negligence that re-
sulted in the child's being quadriplegic, blind, and afflicted with repetitive seizures. The award consisted of $2+ million for general
damages to the parents, $5+ million for damages to the child (R.S.),
and $4.3 million for future expenses and loss of income. Critical to
the verdict was the position taken by the plaintiff that the holiday
skeleton staff arrangement permitted the disaster to occur. "[R.S.]
would have been normal if the hospital had had an adequate number
of staff . . . on the Independence Day holiday."

Case 2.   Dr. K. T., an internist, had his hospital privileges revoked
and was reported to the Medical Disciplinary Board for repeatedly

assuming charge of hospitalized patients and then leaving town for two or three days without either making or clarifying arrangements for cross-coverage during his absence. Finally, but only after an emergency arose, the medical staff took definitive action on an unacceptable practice tolerated for more than two years.

Case 3. Dr. M. B., a family practitioner, had renewal of his hospital privileges denied because of repeated concerns expressed to both his chief of service and his chief of staff by fellow staff physicians, by the hospital's emergency room staff, and by the hospital's nursing staff. All complained of Dr. B.'s unavailability or failure to respond to calls about his patients' needs in the hospital and in the emergency room. The record of repeated warnings to Dr. B. had been clearly established, and a registered letter of warning had been delivered to his office. While in this situation no negligence action had yet been initiated by any of the patients involved, medical staff was of the strong opinion that only because of their voluntary assistance had litigation not ensued; they eventually decided that the behavior had to cease. They recommended non-renewal of Dr. B's privileges and reported him to the Medical Disciplinary Board.

Case 4. T. J., an 18-year-old male, was seen for acute onset of nausea, vomiting, and abdominal pain which localized in the right lower quadrant. Admitted to the hospital, he was observed and had x-ray examination of his abdomen, with no abnormalities being evident, and a complete blood count, which was within normal limits. Given an intravenous fluid and apparently feeling better, he was scheduled to be followed through the night with repeated observations and early morning re-evaluation. During the night his symptoms worsened, and the nursing staff attempted to contact the physician involved, to no avail. So did the family at 7:00 and again at 8:30 A.M.; they, too, were unsuccessful. Finally, the physician appeared at approximately 10:15 A.M., recommended immediate surgery, and later reported that a ruptured appendix was discovered at operation, which would prolong hospitalization several days. Needless to say, both the family and the involved nursing staff were irate and, while no negligence action was initiated, those involved believed the physician's lack of availability precluded his functioning effectively in such situations in the future.

Discussion

Each of these episodes highlights the fact that both the public and the profession have expectations of physicians' individual and group availability significantly higher than a generation ago. As physicians, we must respond to these expectations, or be prepared to suffer the consequences.

Reflect momentarily on what has transpired over the past 20 years and you can recognize some of the events which have been responsible. First and foremost, the U.S. telephone system has achieved its maturity; "beepers," "pagers," and message-recording devices have added to that system, making instant availability at least theoretically possible. These developments were complemented by the emergence of full-time emergency room staffs in urban communities; and, in some communities, it has become increasingly easy for physicians to sign out to the conveniently staffed ER. More and more group practices have implemented and publicized their 24-hour, round-the-clock availability, leading again to increments in the public's expectations.

One also ought to take note of the justifiable interest in the federal government's Emergency Medical Service Program, which sponsored Seattle's now-famous 911 program, providing instant medical access and availability. We all point to it with pride and tout it widely as contributing to lower morbidity and mortality for trauma, burns, and heart attacks. Nowhere is this change in availability more evident than in the field of poison centers: nationwide 24-hour instant availability of ingredient or toxicity information on more than 350,000 trade-name products. Contrast all of this with a generation ago. No doubt failure to live up to the public's high expectations, be they realistic or exaggerated, can be counted on to set the stage for negligence actions in the future.

Lest one reject the concept and its implications, consider for a moment your own hospital. Today, tonight, or this weekend, you expect stat lab tests unimagined a decade ago. If your patient needs a chest x-ray or an EKG at any time, you expect it to be there. These services are available because of planning, planning involving a group and at a significant cost. Without such planning, without such groups, and without the associated costs, chaos exists; with them, coverage follows. Naturally such a coverage involves the group's commitment—no one individual can cover 24 hours a day, 7 days a week,

52 weeks a year. It calls for a schedule to be developed and the participants to accept assignments accordingly. Moreover, the participants must accept the consequences of failure to cooperate, which usually means that they will be fired. Either way, the economic consequences are enormous. Do physicians accept these same premises when working in communities?

Each physician has been and continues to be committed to his or her patients; the public (and we, ourselves) see us as somehow being equally committed to and concerned about the patients we inherit during our schedule of coverage, some of whom don't even have a personal physician. Here is the dilemma: How can we meet such expectations, especially in the absence of a consensus about what needs to be done? We have a significant conceptual hurdle to leap, at a time when economic constraints and competition are stacked against us. Nonetheless, we must succeed.

What You Can Do

In your office, do you provide an example to your staff in promptness, demeanor, and courtesy, in line with their expectations as well as those of your patients? Do you keep to your schedule or are you and your staff constantly having to apologize for being behind? Anderson and colleagues (AMA *Socio-Economic Issues of Health* 1981) confirmed that being kept waiting 30 minutes or more antagonizes a considerable proportion of the population and is to be avoided.

In your hospital, has your staff actually discussed the issue of M.D. availability? Do the staff officers know what the administration and the nursing staff think? Has anyone ever really tried to find out if you have a problem? In your hospital's emergency room, how long does it take the average patient to be seen? Is the waiting time appropriate? Has the medical staff ever considered looking into what happens to patients without a personal physician either there or in the hospital?

Does your county society look at these matters before the fact, or does it wait until complaints from hospitalized patients are received? For example, if your society sponsors an answering service, has it ever looked at the average time lapse until response—by individual doctor?

Our technical skills have grown by leaps and bounds. Have our management skills kept up?

SECTION 29
Terminating Life-Support Mechanisms

Case 1. T. N., a 78-year-old woman with no known relatives, had had a progressively downhill course from degenerative illness. A stroke had left her partially hemiplegic. She had discussed future management choices with her physician, emphasizing "no heroic measures," but she had not completed a "living will." One Sunday morning, she suffered another stroke and was brought to a local emergency room. She was seen there, and a diagnosis of severe neurologic damage was made. Admission arrangements were completed and her personal physician left her under the management of a second physician after discussing the patient's wishes with him.

When her personal physician called the next morning, he learned that in the interim "cardiopulmonary resuscitative measures" had been initiated on at least three occasions and that the patient was then on ventilatory support having been paralyzed with "Pavulon." Her physician was distraught and allegedly instructed the nurse over the phone to disconnect the ventilator immediately. Understandably, she refused to do so; he then went to the hospital and disconnected the equipment himself. As might have been predicted, a report on this action was brought to the attention of many, including the hospital administration, the chief of the medical staff, the county's prosecuting attorney, the media, and eventually the Medical Disciplinary Board. While no malpractice action was instituted, stringent disciplinary measures were imposed and an enormous loss of credibility occurred for all concerned.

Case 2. C. H., a 55-year-old male, developed acute symptoms of bowel obstruction. Emergency surgery was successful in relieving the problem, and the patient was discharged with an ileostomy. Later he returned for an elective "take-down" of the ileostomy, which was completed without any untoward event. Postoperatively, however, C. H. had an acute cardiovascular collapse in the recovery room. He was resuscitated quickly, but over the next 48 hours was judged to have suffered irremedial brain damage. With concurrence of eight members of the family, life-support measures were terminated, and C. H. died.

Although a negligence action was eventually brought against the hospital alleging inadequate nursing staffing of the recovery room, a more significant charge of homicide was subsequently brought against the two physicians involved for the process of "terminating life support systems." Involved in the dispute were the large family who had actually discussed the issue with the patient previous to his operation and supported the approach taken (signing a collective statement to that effect), several other physicians, some of whom were of the opinion that cessation of life support was premature, and an intensive care nurse who disputed the process of not using misting equipment in the ventilator after the plan to cease life support systems had been put into operation—as well as the district attorney's office for the county. Complete details of this case have appeared in AMA News (September 16, 1983); in October 1983, the Appeals Court found unanimously in favor of the defendants (AMA News).

Discussion

Both of the above cases touch on the myriad of issues surrounding the ethical dilemma posed by the option of terminating life support systems. Labeling the conflicting elements with such terms as "death with dignity," "living wills," "natural death," "right to die," "right to live," etc., reveals the ambivalence involved. Some may hope that the resulting problems will simply go away, but they will not. Burgeoning technology has helped create this dilemma; added costs and a new emphasis on individual rights make it all the more evident. What had in previous years been speculative issues available for discussion by philosophers have now become real-life day-to-day events in which we all play a part. Witness the competing social values involved in attempting to resolve the "Baby Doe" issue: the rights of the individual infant, the rights of the parent, and the rights of society. We will all be involved in resolving these problems on a daily basis—and today, not tomorrow or several years in the future. Careful and considerate action is called for.

Currently, physicians in Washington State have been given some guidance in this matter by the Supreme Court. In the spring of 1983, that court heard the case of Ms. Colyer—a 69-year-old woman who had had cardiopulmonary arrest and whose spouse, with the support of the attending physicians, had sought cessation of life-support measures. Eventually the court developed recommendations that we can postulate will continue into the future.

The court held that certain guidelines must be followed:

1. A unanimous concurrence by a "prognosis" board made up of the attending physician and no fewer than two other disinterested physicians, with the relevant qualifications, that the patient's condition is incurable and there is no reasonable medical probability of returning to a cognitive sapient state; or, in the event of a disagreement of the prognosis board, a court decision making such finding by clear and convincing evidence.

2. Court appointment of a guardian for the incompetent person plus appointment of a guardian *ad litem* to represent the best interests of the incompetent person in that proceeding.

3. Appropriate exercise by the guardian of the patient's right to privacy and freedom from bodily invasion, if, in the guardian's best judgment, the patient would have chosen to have the life-sustaining treatment removed if he or she had been competent to make the decision.

4. If required, a court determination of the rights and wishes of the incompetent patient, with a guardian *ad litem* appointed to represent the incompetent patient and to present all relevant facts to the court.

These guidelines are currently available to Washington physicians, but additional guidelines are likely to follow, since considerable discussion will be initiated by the Washington State Medical Association and its representatives over the next years with all parties concerned.

On the national scene, too, this issue and its possible solutions are being debated on a daily basis. Interested physicians, hospital administrators, and many attorneys might wish to avail themselves of a publication, "Deciding to Forego Life-Sustaining Treatment," a production of the President's Commission for the Study of Ethical Problems in Medicine and Biomedical and Behavioral Research. A remarkably readable document, it reviews how we got to where we are and how some states are attempting to find a workable, if not ideal, solution to the problem. Model codes are provided for "natural death acts" and durable powers of attorney, as well as policies and procedures for professional and hospital staff to follow to cope with "do not resuscitate" options.*

Finally, the Risk Management Program has distributed to all chiefs of staff and quality assurance coordinators in Washington's hospitals a new series of "Risk Management Review Units," including one directed at the issue of terminating life-support systems. It ought to prove complementary to a review of the topic being simultaneously distributed by the Washington State Hospital Insurance Trust—the self-insurance program for hospitals—via their "Risk Management Bulletin."

What You Can Do

In your hospital, has your organized medical staff had any review of the issues involved in terminating life-support systems? Are members of the staff acquainted with the expectations of the Medical Executive Committee in this regard? Do your hospital's records document that appropriate steps have been followed? Has anyone inaugurated a discussion with the staff in nursing services—especially those in intensive-care units, recovery rooms, and emergency rooms—to assure that optimum communication takes place among the health professionals involved, as well as between them and the patients and/or relatives? It is wise to remember that Murphy—author of Murphy's Law, "If anything can go wrong it will"—is waiting in the wings to get involved in this arena.

---

*Copies are available from the Superintendent of Documents, U.S. Government Printing Office, Washington, D.C. 20402, Library of Congress Card 83-600503. In addition to these avenues of information, the wsma sponsored a forum focusing on this issue at the 1983 annual meeting. Audio tape cassettes of that productive panel discussion are available from wsma, 2033 Sixth Avenue, #900, Seattle, Washington 98121.

10

Expert-Witness Controversies

Saddled with a heritage of a "conspiracy of silence," today's physicians are measuring up to their responsibilities to testify in malpractice cases. County medical societies and specialty associations are declaring publicly their readiness to provide an expert to either plaintiff or defense to review the evidence and speak out accordingly. All this is a gigantic step forward—save, perhaps, for the issue of the insanity plea where such testimony has all too often bordered on the farcical. Nonetheless, to my mind, the least recognized and least publicized vector in the spread of the malpractice epidemic is the non-expert "expert" witness who is all too willing to speak at a deposition, or in front of a jury, often with misleading or inadequate information. And so often no one calls him or her on it. Encouraged to convert controversy into certainty, these individuals are a threat to reason and rationality as they pontificate for profit to the discredit of us all. Perhaps were such experts appointed by and directly accountable to the courts, distortions might be avoided; such a viewpoint has been advocated by G. D. Lundberg (1984).

When "Experts" Disagree

Case 1.   A. B., a 42-year-old laborer, had been bothered for some 10 years by recurring back problems. During that interval, he had consulted more than 12 different physicians seeking relief. He felt, however, that no lasting remedy had been found. When an acute flareup occurred, a thirteenth physician ordered exploration, then removal of an L3-L4 disc. Once again, temporary relief ensued, but within six months the symptoms recurred. A lawsuit followed. Essential to the plaintiff attorney's position was the "expert testimony" of a general surgeon with no track record of particular training or experience in neurology, neurosurgery, or orthopedics. While the defendant physician ultimately prevailed, it was only after significant, and largely unnecessary, expenditure of time, effort, and money by the defendant physician and the involved carrier.

Case 2.   T. T., a 17-year-old helmet-less rider, suffered a severe head injury and multiple fractures of extremities when his motorcycle went out of control (no mechanical defects were ever detected) and hit a tree. He was transported via a volunteer-manned emergency vehicle to a small rural hospital's emergency room, where first-aid measures were taken. The patient stabilized prior to transfer to Elsewhere General. There, additional problems ensued—multiple infections, peripheral nerve injuries—prior to discharge almost four months later.

Within a year, a lawsuit was filed alleging negligence on the part of the initial physician manning the rural hospital's emergency room. An essential element in the plaintiff's case was the testimony provided by a "big-city expert" from a tertiary-care center. The defense ultimately prevailed, following lengthy litigation. Much of the expert's testimony was discredited, not because of lack of expertise, but because of an obvious lack of familiarity with the case record details, the x-rays taken, and the physical and professional staffing limitations at the site of the original emergency room.

Case 3. C. Y., a 29-year-old male, had a long history of adaptive and behavioral problems, insomnia, headaches, and excessive alcohol use. Consulting his local physician, he later received behavioral modification therapy, supportive counseling, and a prescription for a controlled substance. Over the following months, he not only obtained several authorized refills, but also (apparently) some unauthorized quantities of the controlled substance. Within a year, he was assigned to a narcotic addiction withdrawal program. Subsequently, he brought a malpractice action against his physician, alleging that the treatment itself was responsible for the addiction. A six-digit settlement was eventually arranged, largely the result of "expert testimony depositions" stating that the physician's actions, in part, brought about the addiction. (This position was not supported by Boston Drug Surveillance Program observations of 16,000 postoperative patients treated with controlled substances. That study concluded that the frequency of postoperative addiction was virtually nil.) Some felt the defense was lax in not obtaining more adequate counter expert testimony.

Discussion

Each of these cases shows the impact, for good or bad, that expert witnesses can have on medical malpractice cases. Depending upon one's point of view, the "expert" may be "our star witness" or that "hired gun from California."

Attorneys have long charged the medical profession with a conspiracy of silence to protect members of the physician guild in malpractice cases. Especially over the past decade, notable progress has been made in securing qualified physicians to serve as expert witnesses for both the defense and the plaintiff in cases of purported malpractice. Several county medical societies have worked with local bar associations to assure that, once certain procedural matters have been followed, an expert can be identified who will testify—although not necessarily to the point that either plaintiff or defendant would like to hear. Those familiar with malpractice procedures predict an increasing involvement by expert witnesses. What are some of the points an "expert" ought to establish before agreeing to serve or to testify?

1. Take the task just as seriously as if you were the defendent physician; your testimony may be critical in resolving the issue.

2. Review all records, letters, x-rays, etc., as thoroughly as you can.

3. Identify sites and sources of recognized reference materials to substantiate your point of view.

4. Insist on being informed of expected topics of cross-examination and consult the involved attorney in preparing your remarks.

5. Discuss with that attorney (be it defense or plaintiff attorney) unfavorable as well as favorable information developed by your examination of the patient or of the existent reference literature.

6. Convert to writing the details of your financial arrangement with the attorney— and be prepared to reveal it on the witness stand.

7. Be aware that contrary points of view to your opinion may be voiced, and be familiar with the options involved.

8. Always maintain a fair, polite but firm posture in presenting your testimony.

Conversely, at all costs try to avoid:

1. Acting as an advocate or partisan in the case.

2. Overstating your qualifications or experience.

3. Exaggerating or bluffing; if you don't know, admit it.

4. Showing smugness, cockiness, or overconfidence.

5. Losing your temper.

The attorney seeking your testimony can be a real help in clarifying what is to be expected of you; seek and heed his or her advice. Pay particular attention when a lawyer warns you to answer questions but not to volunteer any additional unrequested information. Sometimes an attorney is not well informed about the technical details, but most of the time you are likely to be exposed for exaggerated or misleading statements.

What You Can Do

In your community, does some medical professional review the testimony of expert witnesses to consider whether qualifications or statements have been exaggerated?

In your hospital, when an "expert" testifies at a hospital staff meeting and the testimony is felt to be faulty, what, if anything, happens?

In your office, are your staff and your colleagues careful about not exaggerating either their or your qualifications to patients and visitors?

What can or ought to be done, either in the courts or the hospitals, to "silence the self-appointed expert"? Brent (1982) has called for scholarly review of expert testimony as a way of assuring its accuracy; would you support such an approach?

SECTION 31
Professional Jousting Poses Problems

Case 1. M. W., a 29-year-old male laborer, had a four-year history of recurrent incapacitating low-back pain that sometimes occurred after strenuous exercise but also sometimes flared up without such exercise. While on a hunting trip, he stepped over a log, stumbled slightly, and was seized again with the back pain. Over the next several days, the pain continued with tingling and weakness developing in his left leg. His primary-care physician referred him to a neurosurgeon. The neurosurgeon suspected a disc, confirmed it by mylography, instituted conservative management for some three weeks (without significant relief of symptoms) and only then advised surgery. Although the procedure was apparently uneventful, the weakness did not subside completely. A limp was still present seven months later, but not enough to curtail employment.

One weekend while doing some home repairs, M. W. cut his hand. His primary physician was away so he visited his local emergency room for suturing and was referred to a general surgeon's office for follow-up. During his visit there, he was somewhat taken aback when the surgeon, hearing of the back history and performing only a cursory examination, remarked that the disc procedure must have been "botched" and that he would be pleased to serve as an expert witness to that effect in any lawsuit. The patient subsequently returned to his primary physician and told him of this conversation. The physician reviewed the situation carefully, assured M. W. that he felt no malpractice had taken place and arranged for a third opinion from a nearby medical center; it confirmed no negligence. The general surgeon, in fact, had a reputation as a self-styled expert and had exhibited this type of behavior in the past.

Case 2. A. T., a 26-year-old male with an admitted chronic drug abuse problem, was transported to an emergency room by his family because of his peculiar behavior. Lethargic, a bit "spacy," and adamant that his problem was largely the result of alcohol rather than drugs, the patient nonetheless was x-rayed and observed for some five hours before being discharged to his family with the admonition that they should not leave him unattended. Unfortunately they did, and the patient was found dead three days later. His death was ruled a suicide caused by drugs consumed after he returned home. The family, however, brought suit alleging that the emergency room physician had been negligent in (among other things) not ordering a variety of lab tests. An expert witness for the plaintiffs testified by deposition that, in such situations, the current standard of practice saw (not "should see") all possible drug overdoses always evaluated by toxic screening, multiple channel EKG, and SMA-12 analysis. Despite testimony to the contrary from a host of other experts, the dispute ended by involving both the courts and the Medical Disciplinary Board before the defendant was exonerated; the expert witness was criticized and censured for his inaccurate and grossly exaggerated comments.

Case 3.   J. M., a 28-year-old female, had been plagued for almost ten years by recurrent mid-line lower abdominal pain for which no explanation was found despite "multiple mega-workups." Varied medical management approaches had been employed with, at most, only temporary benefit. Of note was the fact that at no time did the patient develop any signs or symptoms of drug dependency. Apparently somewhat in desperation, she and her attending obstetrician/gynecologist decided on a hysterectomy; there had, in fact, been two episodes of non-cyclic spotting and physical examination did reveal probable fibroids. The procedure was uneventful and the postoperative course was without any complications, but the pain continued unabated. Consulting still another physician, the patient was somewhat astounded to hear his outspoken criticism of the hysterectomy and his suggestion that she strongly consider instituting a malpractice action. In this instance, rather than pursue such a course of action, she returned to her initial physician and is currently filing a grievance against the second physician with the county medical society.

Discussion

Each of these cases demonstrates one or another ramification of what Colorado's medical malpractice consultant Dr. Bob Britain refers to as "professional jousting." As the cases are presented, each would appear to indict one or more physicians for inappropriate behavior. Although extenuating circumstances might have been present, they were not investigated by the accusing physician. That physician, it would seem, spoke out of turn.

Every physician has been faced with patients whose care by another physician appears to have been less than ideal. Occasionally that care may border on, if not actually constitute, bona fide medical malpractice. In such situations, the responsible physician cannot in good conscience remain totally silent. The physician would want to be assured that the facts of the case are actually as they have been represented; he or she might wish to examine the medical record itself or contact the other physician directly before proceeding further. Often it is helpful to discuss the issue with a trusted colleague; that process can help organize one's thoughts and clarify the options available.

Perhaps the concerned physician will then proceed to some action such as filing a grievance with the county medical society, bringing a complaint to the hospital medical staff, dispatching a letter of concern to the Medical Disciplinary Board, or approaching the patient directly. The point is that the concerned physician ought not, as an initial action, pit the patient against the other physician.

As most readers know, the medical profession is full of rumors and innuendoes about allegedly erroneous statements provided by physician "experts" or "non-expert experts" at depositions or in front of juries. Some defense attorneys prefer to treat such statements as isolated events and seek to refute the arguments presented by discrediting the witness. Others would favor, not the exclusion of the expert's testimony, but publicity of his or her performance throughout the professional community, the county medical society, or the hospital's medical staff, so that appropriate peer pressure might serve as some source of corrective action. Still others suggest more stringent action, i.e., filing grievances with county societies or complaints with the Medical Disciplinary Board. It well might be that action by the Medical Disciplinary Board would prove of benefit; certainly all eyes will be on the Board as it reviews the record of malpractice cases now being brought to it under its mandatory reporting requirements. For emphasis, the focus of concern is limited to inaccurate, erroneous, or inflated statements as they may be provided by any expert, not just those for the plaintiff but also those for the defendant.

In years gone by, individual physicians and organized medicine have been accused of a "conspiracy of silence." By and large that accusation has fallen by the wayside. The profession today has accepted its obligation to expose incompetent behavior; it seeks to assure that experts are available to both plaintiff and defense attorneys—and ought to take steps to ensure that their tesimony is accurate. To accomplish this objective, medicine would do well to monitor such testimony to assure that the experts see themselves as being fully accountable for their performance, both in the courtroom and in front of their peers.

What You Can Do

In your hospital, when evidence of professional jousting is found, what happens? Which, if any, hospital committee becomes involved? How are recurrences prevented? When or if a liability action is concluded against either the hospital or a member of the medical staff, does the case get reviewed? By whom? Are the details publicized?

Do aggrieved patients *know of* (not simply have available) an avenue to formally register complaints? Do they use it? How do you know that they know?

Certainly, much of the malpractice scene will remain an adversary area; even more certainly, if the issue is to be even partially resolved more objective approaches must be found in terminating disputes and assuring that appropriate expert witnesses are involved.

SECTION 32

Non-Expert "Expert" Witnesses

Case 1. R. W., a 39-year-old male laborer, had been bothered off and on by low back pain for more than a decade. Seen by a succession of physicians—family practitioners, internists, radiologists, orthopedists, neurologists, and three neurosurgeons—he eventually underwent two operations to correct his "disc problem." Unfortunately, neither provided any lasting relief. After more than a year of being confined to bed, he brought action against the second operator (an orthopedist) alleging that the type of procedure employed was outmoded, antiquated, and inappropriately performed, and that it had been superseded by a far more effective procedure. Surprisingly, this stance was enthusiastically supported by the "expert testimony" of a general surgeon who, on cross-examination, admitted to having never personally conducted the procedure, having learned about it at a refresher course on a two-week stint in Chicago. Fortunately, the defendant physician was eventually exonerated, but the "expert" continued to be undaunted in his convictions and in his willingness to testify.

Case 2.   Y. C., a 30-year-old obese (285-pound) female, visited her physician in his office because of non-localized abdominal pain. At that point, her history was non-contributory; the medical record documented that the physical examination revealed diffuse abdominal tenderness, but normal bowel sounds and a negative rectal examination; laboratory findings included a white count of 14,500 with a shift to the left; voided urinalysis was normal. Observed briefly in the office, she was then transferred to a hospital emergency room for x-ray (which was read as negative by her physician); she was admitted and permitted clear fluids overnight, with an order to be seen by a surgeon in the morning. At that time, abdominal distention was obvious, bowel sounds were decreased, and the x-ray was reinterpreted as indicative of ileus, which on repeat x-ray was confirmed. After undergoing surgery for a suspected ruptured appendix, she had a relatively uneventful postoperative recovery, save for a minor wound abscess which accompanied the drain. Nonetheless, and supported by "expert testimony" from a teaching center, a suit was brought against the family physician and the general surgeon involved. Again on cross-examination, the situation eventually was clarified but at significant cost to all involved.

Case 3.   C. W., a five-day-old male infant, had arrived via normal vaginal delivery at home following his mother's uneventful pregnancy (her third), during which she had sought no prenatal care. At the last moment, she contacted a nurse midwife (who had a supervising physician) to assist a home delivery. C. W. did well until Day 3, when he was noted to be slightly jaundiced; on Day 4 he was brought to the physician's office, where a serum bilirubin was ordered. Subsequently, the child was admitted to a hospital for diagnosis and treatment. By the time of arrival, the bilirubin had reached 31 mg percent. Mother-baby studies excluded an Rh problem, but established an ABO set-up. Therapy was conducted uneventfully, with a normal recovery.

After the child was admitted to the hospital, there was considerable staff hostility toward the mother and the involved physician. At least two letters were sent to the county medical society's grievance committee calling for a hearing on the physician's "totally inadequate care." When the facts were eventually clarified, both letters were withdrawn. But again, the "expert testimony" had caused some unpleasantness, significant costs, and lengthy discussions—because of pre-existing bias.

Discussion

The foregoing cases are but three samples of an ever-increasing problem of "expert testimony." Pogo (Walt Kelly's comic-strip character) is credited with the expression "We have met the enemy and it is us." That aphorism is particularly applicable to the malpractice scene, especially where such problems as "professional jousting," "specialty puffery" and "nonexpert-expert testimony" are seen so frequently. A recent risk management meeting of physicians' health insurance programs stressed that solutions to these problems do not entail legislative action, insurance company participation, or legal intervention. Rather, solutions must emerge from within the profession itself. Several recent publications stress that point.

Two acknowledged malpractice authorities, Gots and Gots emphasize the need for "physicians—those normally dubbed as 'plaintiff or defense regulars'—[to] support claims that are supportable!" They go on to recommend that "clinical skepticism" be resurrected during practice so that experts are forced to do their homework. Along the same lines, many practitioners decry the reluctance of qualified physicians to participate in the legal process. "By not participating in the litigation process, the vacuum created is filled with a group of 'regular defense or plaintiff' physician expert witnesses whose testimony is purchased by attorneys obtaining a predictable biased viewpoint."

Perhaps the most telling statement is in a recent paper by Brent in *Pediatrics* (November 1982) entitled "The Irresponsible Expert

Witness: A Failure of Biomedical Graduate Education and Professional Accountability." In his opinion, a number of factors contribute to the rise in malpractice cases. He feels unbelievable examples of "inappropriate" (i.e., outrageous) expert testimony have occurred in court cases dealing with radiation exposure and its consequences. In some instances, that testimony has not been refuted by cross-examination. Brent advocates, as an approach to solving the problem:

1. Initiating educational programs by medical and graduate schools about the expert's function, which are directed at the full range of professional students, including some academicians themselves.

2. Considering depositions and court testimonies as "scholarly endeavors," with on-top-of-the-table, before-the-fact consultation and discussion rather than simply complaints after the fact.

3. Reconsidering the economics of expert testimony to assure that the "secretive, moonlighting" nature of some professional testimony is exposed.

4. Clarifying the qualifications of the expert in all instances before the court so that the individual who is not qualified to speak as a provider of care is not permitted to testify.

5. Encouraging the publication of review articles about actual testimony that has been given in the court and found erroneous.

Despite the problems, all is not simply black and white. Formerly, physicians testified for neither the defense nor the plaintiff in court. While perhaps the pendulum has swung too far in the other direction, it's no cause for a return to non-cooperation as an appropriate solution. In contrast, some parties urge that erroneous expert testimony be published in local county medical society bulletins for review by peers so that peer pressure is directed at correcting the problem. Getting the information out in the open would in itself be remarkably beneficial.

What You Can Do

In your community, do you and your colleagues stand ready, willing, and able to serve as experts, regardless of whether called on to testify by either plaintiff or defense attorneys? If not, how is such testimony to be arranged? Do they have to bring in "hired guns" from elsewhere?

In your county, do your plaintiff and defense attorneys go out of their way to assure that irresponsible expert testimony is given the light of day?

The medical profession has a responsibility to testify, and a comparable responsibility to assure that testimony is accurate to all extents possible.

11

The Group vs. the Individual M.D.

Possibly the most overlooked or purposely ignored issue in today's malpractice dilemma is the conflict between the rights of the group and those of the individual physician. Dr. A. is forced to purchase malpractice insurance to join the staff at Hospital C and Dr. B. is pushed off the raft by Insurance Company X when he has three losses in two years. Some argue that licensure status as opposed to malpractice insurance protection ought to be the determinant of the opportunity to practice. Others hasten to point out that the licensure mechanism has been too slow or non-responsive to eliminate "bad actors," and that the insurance mechanism is an opportunity to exploit. One point is all too clear: it is not the individual who is the determinant in either case; group action and group accountability are paramount. At present the group seems to be winning, as it apparently invariably does. Candidly, is there an economic alternative?

SECTION 33

Who's Responsible? Hospital vs. M.D.

Case 1. R. A., a 22-year-old male, suffered a compound fracture of his finger while playing basketball. After primitive first aid, he finished the game and in the evening went to a hospital emergency room for definitive treatment. His finger was x-rayed, irrigated, debrided, and sutured by the ER physician. The patient was instructed to visit his own physician in five to six days for suture removal, or sooner should swelling or pain occur. He also was given a copy of the hospital's emergency care instructions. Over the next 48 hours, the patient alleged that swelling and severe pain developed. He said he called the ER twice and was reassured by nurses and he then visited another physician and ER where infection was diagnosed and treated. Later the patient brought suit charges against the first ER physician and against the hospital, claiming negligence and "agency" (the physician was an agent of the hospital), respectively.

The hospital sought and was granted a summary judgment based on its position that the ER physician was not, in fact, its agent. On appeal, however, the judgment was reversed and remanded for further proceedings because, in the opinion of the court, an "ostensible agency relationship" appeared to have existed.

Case 2. E. D., a 19-year-old male, endured a compound fracture of his right tibia as the result of an athletic accident (not a Washington case). Admitted to hospital via the emergency room, he had a cast applied. Within 24 hours, he was complaining of increasing pain in the involved leg and eventually—following detection of cast constriction, vascular compromise, subsequent infection, and amputation—a suit was instituted against both the physician and the hospital. The patient charged that the hospital was negligent because it failed to enforce the medical staff's bylaws (adopted by its Board of Trustees), which called for mandatory orthopedic consultation. The focus of the suit was on failure of the hospital to discharge its management responsibility, even though subsequent extrapolation of that ruling suggests that the court held the hospital responsible for the medical care per se.

Case 3. P. M., a 71-year-old male, was admitted to the hospital for cardiac surgery. During the procedure something happened to the heart pump tubing, resulting in extensive leaking and entry of air into the system. By the time the problem was detected, the stage was set for severe neurologic impairment. The patient's attorney brought suit against both the surgeon and the hospital (as well as the equipment manufacturer), claiming all parties were negligent in the conduct of their respective responsibilities. Since neither the cardiac surgeon nor his employed pump technician were agents of the hospital, the case became controversial because of the question of any liability on the part of the hospital and the presence of two different insurance carriers, each pointing to the other party. The outcome of such controversies in the future will be significant. The court attributed joint liability in this case.

Case 4. K. W., a 29-year-old para 2 gravida 3, was admitted at term to the hospital. Labor progressed slowly. After an "appropriate interval," she was given IV pitocin with an almost immediate increase in the frequency and intensity of contractions. Some two hours later, her obstetrician happened to drop by the labor room on his way to see another patient, only to find that heavy vaginal bleeding was occurring and that the fetal heart rate had dropped to approximately 60. Calling immediately for an anesthesiologist's help, he accomplished a forceps delivery within 10 minutes. The subsequent Apgar scores were 1 and 3, respectively. During the neonatal period the infant remained floppy, evidenced significant respiratory distress and repetitive seizures; neurologic impairment was obvious. Shortly thereafter a malpractice action was instituted, claiming that (1) the physician was responsible for inappropriate use of pitocin; and (2) the hospital was culpable because the labor room staff had failed to adequately monitor and document the progress of labor and the fetal heart rate. Defense attorneys for the respective carriers appeared to take the position that the other party was totally responsible. The settlement established joint responsibility.

Discussion

Each of the above cases involves plaintiffs' actions that are directed against both the physician and the hospital. Such actions are presenting increasing problems. On the one hand, plaintiffs' attorneys seek to take advantage of Willie Sutton's Law ("go where the money is") and claim blame lies in multiple directions. On the other, the physician and his or her carrier and the hospital and its carrier mount respective defenses to point the finger in the other's direction. Such defenses all too often appear to admit that negligence has occurred and that a bad outcome is attributable to it (the essential elements of monetary recovery), but then go on to imply culpability of the other party. The doctor's attorney claims the hospital is responsible and the hospital's attorney reverses the charge. When played in front of a judge or jury, such strategies often simply serve to establish as fact that wrong has been done, when that may not actually be the case. Once such "fact" is accepted, the only task remaining is for the judge or jury to decide which party was "legally responsible" and how much the award should be.

Perhaps as important is the increasingly hard-nosed position hospitals are taking in exerting authority and control over their physicians. Ostensibly this control limits the hospital's liability exposure, but perhaps it serves other purposes as well, such as assuming more control over the practice of medicine, especially its economic aspects.

Looked at historically—and in this instance historically means going back only 30 years—the dilemma is of relatively recent origin. While malpractice actions directed at physicians in the United States go back to the 1790s, they occurred infrequently until after the middle of the twentieth century. Of malpractice actions in the past 200 years, it's said that as much as 90 percent have occurred in the last 15 years. Although the precise numbers are clouded in controversy, malpractice actions are continuing to escalate in exponential fashion. So, too, are the size of awards. The amounts being sought are increasing at a rate of greater than 20 percent per year.

Until recent years, however, hospitals were seldom the targets of negligence actions. Up to the 1960s, many public hospitals (including those created under "hospital district legislation") were considered to be "immune" from allegations of negligence under legal tenets borrowed from old English law: the king was immune from doing wrong and hospitals, being "descendants" of the king (i.e., the state), could also do no wrong. At the same time, church-related hospitals escaped financial culpability under the concept of "charitable immunity." Even today, the federal government retains a halo of immunity. For example, military dependents claiming negligence against government hospitals must first have their cases reviewed before they are granted the "privilege" of bringing suit. Community hospitals and public hospitals, however, enjoy no such advantage as in the past; their reputations and resources are on the line. Successful suits have been brought and sizeable awards have been made.

Perhaps more telling than this evolution in the concept of immunity have been two other important developments. First, the hospital is no longer considered simply a hotel, a protected environment providing bed and board, where the physician plies his or her trade. Were the hospital simply a hotel, it could hardly be held negligent for anything, save perhaps for the consequences of falls or slippage down flights of stairs. Today, however, the hospital is seen as a hotbed of modern technology and professional services over and above the physicians' services. Untoward events can and do occur, and the consequences can be disastrous and costly. The hospital can thus be seen as responsible and potentially negligent.

Second, in many jurisdictions, physicians are no longer independent contractors free to come and go and ply their trade in the hospital. Rather, the physician is viewed as an essential cog in the hospital, for which the hospital (as a corporate body) has increasing amounts of responsibility even though it doesn't pay his or her salary. When the hospital does pay the salary or when it does provide precise direction, it accepts the implication of a "master-servant" relationship. If a mistake occurs, it is the master who is responsible. As an example, in operating rooms the surgeon may no longer be recognized as the captain of the ship (master) and thus may not be seen as totally responsible for mishaps; this may get him or her off the liability hook for the action of a nurse, for example, but it can create other problems.

In Case 1, even though a detailed contract existed between the emergency room physician and the hospital, even though the physician was not salaried, and even though the hospital had no direct managerial say over the physician's actions, the court ruled that an agency relationship appeared to exist and that patients visiting the emergency room certainly had no reason not to think the emergency room physicians were agents of the hospital. As a consequence, the hospital's potential opportunity for directing the actions of its physicians can be seen as growing daily.

Stimulated by the decision in *Darling v. Charleston Community Hospital* in the mid 1960s (as illustrated in Case 2), the courts have increasingly ruled the hospital corporate structure to be ultimately responsible for everything that goes on in the hospital. Some would add that more than an occasional board member, more than an isolated administrator, and more than a rare governmental bureaucrat have encouraged such conceptual change. Others would point out that more than one physician and certainly much of organized medicine has resisted this conceptual change. While one could argue the pros and cons of such polar positions, on a day-to-day basis, both players—the hospital and the physician—must work together to prevent problems leading to allegations of malpractice. Joint risk management programs are essential. Without the cooperation of the hospitals, physicians' efforts in risk management will fall far short of the mark. Without the physicians' cooperation and active participation, hospitals will find themselves similarly frustrated while expending more and more dollars and effort in ineffectual programs.

What You Can Do

In your hospital, is there an identifiable risk management program with participation by hospital and by medical staff? Does the involved committee meet during working hours (when physicians tend not to come) or during the evening hours (when hospital staff tend to be absent)? Do physicians step forward to identify problems and institute corrective action, such as insisting that charts be signed and operative notes be dictated, or do they band together in "collective foot-dragging"?

Are problems seen as the doctor's problem or the hospital's problem or as "our" problem? Many hold that only by seeing them as "our problems" will we be able to achieve significant improvements in professional liability prevention in the future.

SECTION 34

Failure to Enforce Staff Bylaws

Case. Having symptoms of progressive aortic and femoral arterial incompetence, D. K., a 64-year-old female, sought care through her family physician and was eventually referred to Dr. S., a vascular surgeon. After dye studies confirmed occlusive problems, she was admitted to the hospital for prosthetic surgery. Postoperative thrombotic and other complications ensued, which resulted in the eventual loss of her leg from just above the knee. Shortly thereafter, liability actions were brought against both Dr. S. and the hospital.

The action directed at the physician alleged negligence in the strategy and conduct of the procedure itself, and in the management of the complication. After considerable review of the issues, a settlement of approximately $300,000 was reached.

The action directed at the hospital alleged negligence, not in the technical care of the patient, but in the hospital's failure to enforce the administrative policies, procedures, and decisions of its medical staff and administration. Because of prior intra- and postoperative problems, Dr. S. had been brought to the attention of the hospital and medical staff authorities. An oral agreement had been reached that the surgeon would refrain from any additional aortic-femoral vascular procedures until a full review of the situation had been completed by the appropriate medical staff committee.

Approximately two months later, prior to the completion of the review, the operating room supervisor reported to the hospital administrator that K. D. had been admitted to the hospital by Dr. S. and was scheduled for the specific procedure at issue. The administrator tried to reach the chief of staff but failed; he then talked with the chief of surgery, who, upon hearing the patient was already admitted and was on the schedule for that day and being familiar with the details of the previous problems, granted a non-emergency exception to the restriction of Dr. S.'s surgical privileges.

As noted above, a bad outcome was the result. Despite a vigorous defense, a jury found for the plaintiff against the hospital in the amount of $2.1 million! The reasoning was enunciated precisely: failure to enforce the policies and procedures stipulated in the hospital and medical staff bylaws, rules, and regulations. An appeal is under consideration.

Discussion

Many experts predict this type of problem will serve not only as a significant source of negligence claims in the near future, but also as a pivotal point of possible controversy between the hospital and the individual physician and/or the medical community. The issue at hand is clearly one of the transfer of authority, power, and control from the physician to the hospital, and all its implications, including corporate responsibility.

Before the mid-1960s and despite lip service to the contrary, the individual physician was the dominant influence on the U.S. hospital scene. The concept of corporate conscience was at a very embryonic stage in hospitals as well as in medical organizations. A license to practice medicine and surgery sufficed in many instances to undertake virtually any medical or surgical procedure, in or out of the hospital. Moreover, a poor outcome, or series of poor outcomes, were unlikely to be followed by any corporate censure by the hospital, medical organizations, disciplinary boards, or even the courts. Things have changed!

Paramount in this change was the landmark *Darling vs. Charleston Community Hospital* decision discussed earlier in which a young athlete's fractured leg had to be amputated following vascular compression from casting. The court held that the patient was entitled to a sizeable award because the hospital had failed to enforce its medical staff-approved and board of trustees-endorsed policies and procedures mandating consultation in such cases. The simple fact that the consultation did not take place was sufficient to convince the court of corporate negligence.

During the past several years, other jurisdictions have reached numerous comparable conclusions in holding hospitals vicariously liable by this line of reasoning for the negligence of their medical staffs. It has, then, become increasingly clear that the medical staff and the hospital have an obligation to the public to develop policies and procedures to safeguard that public. This includes not only the technical conduct of laboratory tests and operations, but also the technical competence of its medical staff members. Moreover, this concept of corporate responsibility was expanded in New Jersey's *Corleto v. Shore Memorial Hospital* which found the hospital, each member of the hospital's board, and its entire medical staff, and the administrator liable for damages resulting from the actions of one surgeon.

After first understanding and then accepting the theory of corporate responsibility, each individual physician will want to ensure the development and enforcement of appropriate policies and procedures in the various professional organizations to which he or she belongs. In essense, the pursuit of such innovations is behind many of the activities of the Joint Commission on Accreditation of Hospitals. If successful, such endeavors will serve to better protect the public and insulate both the physician and the hospital from allegations of corporate negligence.

What You Can Do

In your hospital, do the medical staff bylaws, policies, and procedures provide for the restriction/revocation of staff privileges? Do they assure fairness and due process? Are you sure? One prominent Seattle hospital found that they didn't—after the fact. If a physician's privileges are limited in scope, just how is that limitation monitored? What mechanisms, if any, assure that the appropriate consultations occur in your intensive care unit, your coronary care unit, your operating room, or in your emergency room?

Finally, just how good is the screening of qualifications by your Credentials Committee for new applicants? Or, perhaps more telling, is the annual re-evaluation of the practices of present members prior to reappointment adequate?

Obviously, tight compliance with the called-for detailed documentation is an enormous task for voluntary staff members of community hospitals. Isn't the value of compliance so high that the medical management required ought to be reimbursed? Some progressive hospitals are, in fact, putting their money into such projects. Is yours?

SECTION 35

The Consequences of Uninsured M.D.s

Case 1. R. G., a 46-year-old female, was admitted to hospital with symptoms of recurrent right upper abdominal discomfort of approximately two years' duration. Cholangiography confirmed the presence of multiple stones; except for moderate obesity, the remainder of the physical and laboratory examinations were all within normal limits, as was an EKG. Scheduled for elective cholecystectomy, R. G. experienced no intraoperative problems, but her postoperative course was complicated by a series of wound and intra-abdominal infections, all believed to have stemmed from the surgical procedure. Retrospectively, issue was taken with the recommendation of the infectious disease consultant regarding the choice of antibiotics. Eventually a malpractice action was brought against three defendants: the operating surgeon, the infectious disease consultant, and the hospital. Only the first and the last had any liability insurance coverage in place. While eventually the case was adjudicated without any financial settlement whatever, considerable jockeying for defensive position had taken place among the three defendants, with long-term detrimental outcomes to all.

Case 2.   T. N., a 13-year-old male always in good health, developed progressively severe abdominal pain commencing in the region of the umbilicus and gradually moving to the right lower quadrant. It was accompanied by nausea and later by vomiting. His parents attempted to contact their regular physician whose answering service was unable to reach him on a Saturday afternoon. Because the symptoms worsened, T. N. was brought to the community hospital's emergency room in the evening where he was examined, had a plain abdominal film (with the fecalith being visible), and a CBC with elevated WBC (16,800 and a shift to the left). He was referred to a surgeon who saw him and scheduled him for surgery some two hours later. When he was examined by the surgeon, symptoms had progressed and a probable ruptured appendix was diagnosed.

Later the parents alleged that the surgeon was highly critical of their regular physician who had been "unavailable," and added that had T. N. been seen earlier, the rupture probably could have been avoided. T. N. went to the operating room shortly after midnight and, indeed, a ruptured appendix was found. Appendectomy and drainage were performed; antibiotics and IV fluids were initiated; and the patient returned to the floor about 2:00 A.M. Seen the next morning by his usual physician, T. N. was felt to be progressing "well," but the physician changed an antibiotic order, expressing to the parents (according to them) an opinion that the initial choice of antibiotics had been less than ideal. Unfortunately, T. N. went on to develop a significant peritonitis which required almost ten days of hospitalization, followed by recurrent abdominal pain with subsequent re-exploration some three months later for removal of "intestinal adhesions." T. N.'s parents were less than satisfied with the extended course of illness, and brought suit against both the surgeon and the physician involved. The hospital and the emergency room physician were excluded. Unfortunately, one of the two defendants' attorneys attempted to arrange that his uninsured client's case be dropped from the allegation so that the involved insurance carrier would be accountable for the brunt of the problem. The outcome was a financial judgment against the carrier.

Case 3. B. C., a 60-year-old male, presented to his family physician with signs and symptoms of prostatic hypertrophy; he was referred for a urologic work-up (including x-rays), at the conclusion of which a prostatectomy was performed without complications. Microscopic section of the removed tissue was interpreted as indicating carcinoma; radiation and cancer chemotherapy were instituted. Subsequently some degree of sexual impotency occurred, and the patient had another work-up. Re-examination of the removed tissue led to a conclusion that there was, in fact, no carcinoma. An allegation of malpractice was instituted against multiple defendants claiming that inappropriate therapy had been undertaken. All but one of the defendants had insurance, and in the end only the insureds paid.

Discussion

These three cases emphasize that today's physician has a vested interest in knowing the liability insurance status of his or her colleagues—as well as of his or her hospital. The existing policy of Washington's Hospital Insurance Trust, which currently insures almost all of this state's hospitals, is to require that the insured hospitals in turn require that their staff physicians document their liability insurance. Similarly, carriers insuring groups of physicians expect all members of a group to participate. Interestingly, it has been the hospitals and the carriers and not the medical profession who have pushed this point in Washington State.

For a glimpse into the future, it pays to look at California. Only in 1974 did their legislature pass a statute making it "legal" for a hospital to require malpractice insurance for any member of its medical staff, new or old. Supporting the need for such a requirement is a subsequent 1978 California Supreme Court decision affirming "the doctrine of complete joint and several liability" for all liable defendants. As a consequence, if one defendant cannot pay his or her "comparative indemnity," the other defendants must pick up the tab together. Such a position virtually assures that lawyers, on the basis of the "deep pocket theory," will try to identify multiple parties, including the hospital, as defendants in any malpractice action. This guarantees that payment will be made. Both in Oregon and in California this doctrine of shared liability has been upheld by the courts.

Anticipating another malpractice crisis on the horizon, the California Medical Association surveyed both the chiefs of staffs of California hospitals and a representative sample of California Medical Association members in late 1981 to seek their understanding of just where hospitals stood on this point. In the middle of the 1970s, the California Hospital Association had strongly supported the concept of mandatory insurance; more recently they had abandoned their very strong position and left it to local option. The California Medical Association counsel in addition had expressed an opinion that a court might conceivably overrule the requirement if the cost of the insurance to a remote-practice practitioner were too high.

Of note is the finding of the survey that only 56 percent of California's 390 hospitals had actually adopted the position of requiring liability insurance. For some reason, however, 71 percent of the California Medical Association members themselves perceived that they were, in fact, required to have malpractice insurance as a condition of accepting staff membership. The reason for this discrepancy in perception remains unclear; by and large, it would seem to be a favorable "misconception" from the vantage point of the majority of California's physicians. Nonetheless, a significant number of physicians in California do remain "bare"—making a risk for all of their colleagues. Looked at objectively, physicians have enough risk as individuals; it makes little sense to subsidize a colleague who chooses to save the premium costs.

What You Can Do

Does your hospital require both old and new members of your medical staff to document their insurability status regarding malpractice? If no, why not? If yes, who actually validates and verifies the class and conditions of the insurance? Are you sure?

Does your hospital condone any physician serving in the emergency room without evidence of malpractice insurance? Some permit "emergencies" to supervene, at a risk to both the institution and the colleague physicians. In your community what is being done to assure that all such physicians do have appropriate professional liability coverage?

The costs of liability insurance are high; for the occasional individual who goes without, it's simply a matter of shifting costs to the rest of the physician population, and to their patients. What, actually, is the status of "bare physicians" in your state? The issue poses a concern to all the insurers who may be forced to cover loses. Conclusion: stay insured.

Clarification of Corporate Negligence

Case.   M. P., a 33-year-old multipara, became ill during the thirty-fifth week of her pregnancy, with a headache and notable edema in her lower extremities. Visiting her physician's office on two consecutive days, she was found to be hypertensive and was allegedly sent home on a treatment regimen of bed rest and aspirin. Unfortunately, two days later she was admitted to a Washington hospital in a comatose condition under the care of another physician. She was taken to surgery following a diagnosis of irreversible cerebral death due to an intracranial hemorrage, and her child was delivered by Cesarean section. Subsequently (1978), with the family's consent, respiratory support was discontinued and she died.

A negligence action was brought against the original treating physician, Dr. D., by M. P.'s estate. In addition, a second negligence action was brought against the hospital, arguing that it "violated the duty of care owed Ms. M. P. to grant hospital admitting and treating privileges only to those physicians who were competent." The plaintiff based his allegations on the theory of "corporate negligence" as it applies to Washington's hospitals, and the purported responsibilities it implies. The hospital sought a summary judgment in its favor, which was granted by the Superior Court. On appeal up through the State Supreme Court, that decision was affirmed and the hospital was judged not to be in any way culpable for the disastrous outcome.

Discussion

This case is of special significance to all concerned with health care services. The critical, but until the time of this decision fuzzy, issue of hospital corporate negligence was under consideration. In its decision the Washington Supreme Court notes that "we hereby adopt the theory of corporate negligence," and it goes on to indicate how such a position is "indeed entirely compatible with prior decisions in our state (the Pederson and the Osborn decisions) and is in concert with the conclusions of virtually all non-Washington jurisdictions which have considered the issue over the past decade."

The important issue for both physicians and hospitals is the court's initial elaboration of what it considers to be the "standard" against which a hospital's performance will be measured. It would seem that hospitals are now expected to abide not just by local standards, but also by national norms—such as those of voluntary groups like the JCAH—as well as the standards set in its own bylaws. The question appears to be whether the hospital adopts policies and procedures to serve as a reasonable basis for credentialing its medical staff and for monitoring that staff's performance.

The court notes that the now-famous *Darling* decision of the mid-1960s was predicated on the hospital's failure to abide by the requirements of its own bylaws, calling for mandatory consultation. The hospital was not judged to be responsible in any supervisory capacity for its member physicians' performances. For both parties, hospitals and physicians, this distinction would seem to be critical. A corporate hospital must have policies and procedures which are actively pursued in seeking quality medical care. The corporate hospital does not practice medicine per se and does not stand in a *respondeat superior* position over its medical staff members. In day-to-day terminology, if the prudent hospital fails to search out and detect obvious discrepancies in Dr. X's application for staff privileges, it is guilty of corporate negligence. In contrast, if, after a thorough search of his credentials, it selects Dr. Y, and if it continues to provide prudent monitoring of Dr. Y's activities, and if in subsequent years Dr. Y is "negligent" in his operative technique or his diagnostic investigations of an individual patient, the hospital is in no way guilty of "corporate negligence."

It is particularly noteworthy that in the case under discussion the plaintiff himself did not claim that the hospital was liable for the negligence of its physician staff member. Instead the plaintiff argued that the hospital, simply by granting privileges to the doctor, failed in its duty to warn M. P. "as a foreseeable patient" of the physician's potential professional shortcomings. It is interesting that the plaintiff did not charge the hospital with being vicariously liable for the negligence of Dr. D. under the theory of *respondeat superior*. The court emphasized that the hospital's duty does not extend outside of its premises: "it does not hold itself out as an inspector or an insurer of private office practice of its staff members."

Suffice it to say that this is not likely to be the final chapter in the continuing saga of hospital staff privileges. The issue is a particularly "hot" topic. Consider the December 1983 AMA House of Delegates meeting, where house staff were concerned about the threat of being frozen out of hospital staff activities. There are also concerns about hospital staff privileges for professionals other than physicians, such as podiatrists and psychologists. In addition, there is a concern expressed by Curran in his 1983 *New England Journal* article calling for the blending of hospital and medical staff liability insurance as a technique to minimize insurance losses and to assure more control over individual staff members. And finally, there is the recent U.S. Supreme Court decision that antitrust laws are not violated when a hospital enters into an exclusive contract with anesthesiologists.

What You Can Do

In your hospital, has there been recent reconsideration and review of the policies and procedures for credentialing medical staff members? Are they compatible with national norms, such as those of JCAH? If they are, has anyone checked to see if the procedures are really being followed by the credentials committee and the medical staff organization on a day-to-day basis? Are controversial points verified? Is the graduate degree of the physician applicant verified, or is his current medical license status validated? Is the malpractice insurance requirement—assuming there is one—reviewed and validated as being in effect? And, perhaps of most importance, is the recredentialing process anything other than a rubber stamp?

Physicians may find this issue frustrating, but the frustration is significantly less than that which occurs when oversight is detected and publicized in the press or in the courts. Do your best to make it work.

12

Peer Reviews

Very little meaningful peer review went on in medicine until a generation ago—save when someone blew a very loud and potentially smelly whistle. Short of murder or mayhem or using controlled substances, little called down the judgment of a physician's peers. Shortly after the turn of the century, first in Britain and then in Boston, formal approaches toward what eventually became peer review began to appear. Characteristically, surgeons played a leading role as individuals and then as members of the American College of Surgeons and the Joint Commission of Accreditation of Hospitals. And, in every state, mechanisms for disciplinary action of the wayward physician have arisen and are in place. While still far from perfect, the peer review mechanism is at least crawling, if not yet up and running. In Washington and a number of other states, both legislative action and supreme court reviews have established that, provided peer review is conducted by an appropriately designated committee of the hospital staff or medical group, its deliberations and conclusions are not subject to "discovery"; this posture goes a long way toward insuring that quality assurance programs of peer review as advocated by the JCAH will remain viable and can prove productive. Today the picture is clear as the profession responds to the choice, "Do it yourself or have the government do it for you."

151

SECTION 37

Peer-Review Programs

Case 1.   Dr. K. S., a board-certified orthopedic surgeon, was a defendant in two separate malpractice cases over a span of three years. In both cases it was alleged that he mistakenly operated on the wrong extremity. A WSMA Claims Review Panel reviewed both incidents and agreed that Dr. S. had been negligent and so advised the insurance carrier. After settlements were arranged, the involved physician was given two options: (1) accept responsibility for the first $50,000 of his next potential loss (that is, agree to a "deductible clause"), or (2) seek insurance elsewhere. He chose the former course and lives with a "deductible" hanging over his head.

Case 2.   Dr. S. T., a generalist in practice for more than thirty years, was a defendant in at least five separate malpractice claims over those years. In considering renewal, the Professional Review Committee concluded that significant problems did exist with this physician's surgical training, his technical competency, as well as his clinical judgment, and recommended he be given the following options: (1) refrain from practicing as an operating surgeon or assisting surgeon in any operating room, and not be on the rotation for emergency room coverage, or (2) look elsewhere for liability insurance coverage. He chose the former course of action.

Case 3.   Dr. K. F., a middle-aged internist, was brought before the Medical Disciplinary Board on charges of repetitive alcohol abuse which interfered with his practice. After a thorough hearing of the facts, the Board provided the physician with two options: (1) undertake a program of total abstinence from alcohol, participate in Alcoholics Anonymous two times per week, and participate in a random sampling program one to two times per week to determine the possible presence of any blood alcohol, or (2) forfeit his license to practice medicine. He chose the former, with twelve months successfully monitored compliance to date.

Case 4. Dr. B. W., age 39, had practiced pediatrics in three states other than Washington and had been involved in both grievance and malpractice allegations in each. Considering re-entry into practice in Washington, he applied for malpractice coverage. After thorough investigation of his practice over the years, the WSMA Professional Review Committee recommended against coverage under the WSMA-sponsored program; the sponsored insurance carrier agreed and denied the application.

Case 5. Dr. W. C. practiced in an urban Washington community for many years providing obstetrical and abortion services. Increasingly, concerns were expressed by her obstetrical and nursing colleagues and by several of her patients that her practice was significantly behind the times, her technique was borderline, and her clinical judgment and interpersonal behavior left much to be desired. Considered by both the county medical society grievance committee and the Medical Disciplinary Board, she was given the option of either undertaking an elaborate update of her knowledge and professional manner or of having her license revoked. She chose gracefully to retire.

Discussion

Each of these cases has its actual basis in fact, with only minor modification to preserve the anonymity of the individuals involved. These vignettes emphasize that, as is true nationally, the state of Washington is experiencing far more peer review, action and follow-up in attempts to upgrade the quality of day-to-day medical practice, protect the public, and curtail medical malpractice lawsuits. The following are key components of that effort:

1. WSMA Claims Review Panels. Four medical association-sponsored panels are operating across the state. Composed of representative specialists and generalists, each meets on a monthly basis and usually considers three cases of possible malpractice at each session. The panel recommends to the doctor, his attorney, and the insurance carrier that a case be defended, settled, or compromised. It also decides whether further investigation into a case by the Professional Review Committee is warranted.

2. WSMA Professional Review Committee. This medical association

committee was created to review the insurability of all new applicants as well as any physician referred to it by the Claims Review Panel, county medical society, hospital medical staff, or insurance carrier. To date the committee has taken a variety of actions, including recommending cancellation or non-renewal of policy, a 200 percent premium surcharge, or limitation of practice. Their decision at times is for no action at all. If a serious problem with a physician comes to light during the review process the committee may refer the physician, via its parent Professional Liability Insurance Committee, to the Medical Disciplinary Board.

3. Washington State Medical Disciplinary Board. The Board is a state agency composed of physicians elected from each Congressional District and a public member appointed by the governor. Its mission is to protect the public and to discipline physicians when appropriate, vindicate them if deserved, or declare them impaired or disabled as called for. A 1977 study of physicians licensed in Washington revealed that 4 percent had had a formal malpractice action brought against them. In contrast, of those physicians who had been brought before the Medical Disciplinary Board, 45 percent had had a malpractice claim brought against them!

Recently adopted Medical Disciplinary Board regulations require that hospital medical staffs, medical societies, third-party payers, and malpractice insurance carriers report final disciplinary actions taken regarding a physician's professional behavior, flagrant over-charging, or a malpractice settlement or judgment in excess of $30,000. In short, all instances in which a serious problem to a patient's welfare might exist must be reported. The Board intends to involve local physicians and medical societies in resolving the issues detected, preferably without the Board's always having to assume an adversary role and particularly in the area of monitoring corrective programs.

The *Wall Street Journal* carried front-page headlines on May 1, 1981, proclaiming, "States move to catch incompetent doctors . . . difficult to get MDs to blow the whistle even with 'snitch laws.'" The message was clear: only a few states are seen as having actually attempted to address this problem, apparently because physicians themselves don't want to get involved. However, attention to due-process resolution of incompetent practices—not always an easy matter—serves to improve the quality of care, protect the public, and keep down the costs of malpractice judgments.

What You Can Do

Ask yourself the following questions, then raise them at your county medical society and hospital-medical staff meetings.

In your hospital, has there been real attention paid to the risk management component of the now JCAH-required "Quality Assurance Plan," or is it simply a pro forma exercise? Is your medical staff prepared to "blow the whistle" when evidence of a poor practice is uncovered, or does it get "stonewalled"?

In your medical society, is a grievance committee actively investigating and hearing complaints brought to it?

Remember: The only real avenue available to keep down your ultimate malpractice costs is via malpractice prevention. Do your part to assure your community's physicians' participation.

SECTION 38

"Fairness" and Due Process

Case 1. Dr. J. J., a generalist with a commitment to "preventive medicine" and "natural remedies," was accused of unprofessional conduct by the Washington Medical Disciplinary Board. Among other things, he allegedly recommended the use of coffee enema in managing several patients with malignancies. Eventually brought before the Disciplinary Board, Dr. J. and his attorney attempted to mount a defense by presenting testimonials and philosophic expositions supporting the technique employed. During a series of hearings, the doctor's attorney took the position that members of the Board, sitting as "jurors," had actually been prejudiced by pre-hearing discussions of details of the case and that the Board's hearing procedures failed to give his client a "fair shake." Nonetheless, the Board completed its hearing and found Dr. J. guilty of unprofessional conduct and revoked his license. That decision was appealed to the Washington Court of Appeals and eventually—two years later—the Court of Appeals ruled that the appeal carried and that while the Board's overall action stood, its *modus operandi* had to change.

Case 2. Dr. D. A., a Washington dermatologist, had been charged with taking sexual liberties during his examinations of a number of female patients. There was considerable rumor and discussion in his local community and much professional indignation was expressed. During his appearance before the Medical Disciplinary Board, his attorney accused several members of the Board of, in essence, acting as prosecutors rather than jurors. As a consequence, when the Board reached a verdict of revocation, Dr. A.'s attorney appealed to the Superior Court on the grounds that "due process had not been observed." Upon reviewing the transcript of the hearings, the judge apparently agreed. Result: rather than attempt to refute the written record, the Board agreed to a compromise solution—to stay the revocation but limit Dr. A.'s professional activities and monitor his practice. Had due process been followed in the original hearings, the outcome possibly would have been different, and both the public and professional reaction to the peer review process would have been more positive.

Case 3. Dr. T. X. moved to a Washington community, set up a practice, and sought staff membership and consultation privileges at several local hospitals. While his applications were being processed, considerable controversy arose about his qualifications, his competency, and his medical philosophy. Statements unfavorable to Dr. X. and his professional reputation reached the press. Unfortunately, the actual investigation of his background was superficial at best; had it been more thorough, the unfavorable statements would have been substantiated—but in fact they were not. Dr. X. successfully brought suit against detractors and received a financial settlement, which, in the eyes of many, would not have been possible had a proper investigation been conducted and had certain physicians in the community refrained from rash comment.

Case 4. Dr. M. O. had served as a medical staff member at Center General Hospital for almost 30 years, enjoying general surgical privileges. In recent years, locker-room conversation led to rumors of problems about Dr. O.'s surgical judgment as well as his technical competence. When the issue was brought before the hospital's staff executive committee—despite the fact that no patient concerns or complaints had been reported—it chose to drastically curtail Dr. O.'s privileges immediately. Granted the opportunity to appeal only after considerable publicity had been given to his change of status, Dr. O. and his attorney quickly established that: (1) no specific review of any data from his charts or from OR records had been presented to the executive committee to substantiate the expressed concern, and (2) no opportunity had been afforded to Dr. O. to refute the concerns expressed or confront his detractors. Needless to say, the issue rapidly mushroomed into the primary topic of hospital conversation with predictable divisive results. The dispute climaxed when Dr. O. filed a lawsuit; eventually it was settled out of court for a relatively small amount, but damage to the public confidence had already been done.

Case 5. Dr. P. T. had been a member of the surgical staff at a small hospital for some 10 years. He was the subject of a malpractice action, and the hospital was also named in the suit, for allegedly permitting Dr. T. to conduct a non-indicated operative procedure. During the long, drawn-out deliberations that followed, it became evident that the medical staff mechanisms had failed to review staff practices and to document that such reviews actually took place. Simply claiming that since no mortality took place, no problem existed was judged a totally inadequate defense.

The medical staff was deemed responsible for judging the appropriateness of the procedures being carried out on the premises and the hospital was responsible for assuring that the medical staff complied. Both the professional reputation of the hospital as well as its attractiveness as an "insured" to insurance carriers suffered as a consequence of the public and professional outrage that followed.

Discussion

While the details of the final three cases have been modified to assure anonymity of those involved, that is not true of the first two cases. Those are the facts as they occurred—or were perceived to have occurred. Admittedly, none of the cases resulted in a large immediate financial loss, but each in its own way has set the stage for such loss and may restrict the evolution of our peer review process.

Because the Court of Appeals' decision in Case 1 has special import, additional details of that decision are presented here. In appealing the Board's decision, Dr. J. J.'s attorney contended that the

Board had violated due process, the Washington Administrative Code, and the "appearance of fairness" in its hearings.

In disputing due process, Dr. J. argued that the Board had acted as investigator, prosecutor, and judge, all at the same time. In its review of the records, however, the court felt that "despite some ambiguous comments by Board members," the Board did not prosecute the case, that function was carried out by the assistant attorney general involved.

Similarly, the court found that procedures did not violate the Washington Code, since nothing in the code prohibits pre-hearing consultation by Board members.

But the court did find that the procedures as carried out violated "the appearance of fairness doctrine." In Washington, the [1898] doctrine implies "the principle of impartiality, disinterestedness and fairness." Fully accepting the integrity of the Board members, the court noted that having a single assistant attorney general serve simultaneously as advisor to the Board and as prosecutor of the plaintiff is inconsistent with an appearance of fairness. The court added that its own opinion on fairness would hold for future cases, but emphasized that this ought not be construed as holding all past procedures invalid. The court concluded by encouraging the profession to continue to accept the responsibility for disciplinary functions and emphasized that "its [the court's] focus on the appearance of impropriety ought not be construed as implying that actual impropriety occurred."

As a consequence of this court action, the following will happen:

1. Because Dr. J.'s license is still suspended, Dr. J. will be entitled to a new hearing, most likely in front of a hearing examiner with review of the hearing records by Board members not involved in the original hearings or by pro-tem Board members.

2. The Board and the Attorney General's office will expeditiously establish procedure to avoid repeating the appearance of unfairness. This will invariably increase the cost of conducting Disciplinary Board activities. The Board's costs are not covered by the current re-licensing fees despite the recent increase in the current statutory limit of $35 per year. As a consequence, we should anticipate eventual increase in that re-licensing fee.

3. Each and every medical society and hospital medical staff will

need to carefully review its procedures to assure that the appearance of fairness doctrine is followed and documented in resolving disputes and taking disciplinary actions.

The appropriate body ought to be certain that necessary data are collected and documented, and that due process is assured. As recently occurred in one Washington community, it is all too easy for well-intentioned community physicians to get caught up in a "lynch mob mentality." Cool heads, careful procedures, data documentation, due process, and the appearance of fairness are all imperative, if we are to be successful in our peer review programs.

What You Can Do

In your hospital, do your medical staff bylaws prescribe the procedural steps, including the appeals process, to be implemented when a potential disciplinary problem occurs?

In your community, does your application form for medical society membership and hospital staff privileges include a specific release signed by the applicant to permit the sharing of appropriate disciplinary actions among health organizations, such as hospitals and medical societies, to better protect the public and serve the profession?

In your hospital, does your medical staff organization actually conduct reviews of patient care procedures, to assure not only that fatalities have been avoided but also, just as importantly, that appropriate indications exist for the conduct of such procedures? With such a program, the peer review process—which will prove critical and essential to the conduct of future risk management programs—can be successful. Without it, risk management will be doomed to failure.

SECTION 39

A Decade of Anesthesiologic Problems

Case 1. J. F., a 17-year-old male suffering with an acute episode of abdominal pain, was admitted to the hospital for an appendectomy. During the procedure (which was done under general anesthesia), a perforated appendix was identified. During its removal, intravenous antibiotics were administered rapidly, and within seconds the patient suffered a cardiac arrest. Unfortunately, even though it was detected immediately, the patient did not respond to either routine or extraordinary measures and died. No identifiable explanatory physical abnormalities were detected at post mortem. Immediate concern by all the physicians involved was directed at the tragedy and toward the family. Subsequent concern focused on the question, *res ipsa loquitur?*—Did the incident speak for itself clearly enough to establish that "malpractice" had occurred?

Case 2. K. T., a 28-year-old female, underwent an uneventful fourth pregnancy and delivered without problems, during which time she was managed by epidural spinal anesthesia. The infant was fine, but almost immediately after the anesthetic wore off, the patient began to complain of "shooting pains" down her left leg with episodic periods of numbness there. Symptoms of neurologic damage persisted. The responsible anesthesiologist and obstetrician each reviewed the details of the case and agreed that no deviation from the standard of practice had occurred. During the work-up of the case, however, the copy of the subpoenaed record was determined to have been "altered significantly," making a defense virtually impossible.

Discussion

Note that both of these cases involved an anesthesiologist. The State Specialty Society of Anesthesiology, instead of simply insisting that such instances are "rare as hens' teeth," decided to carefully review the past eleven years' experiences in Washington. Each detectable case file made available by insurance carriers involving an anesthesiologist was reviewed in detail; all records of any medical examiner involving an anesthetic death were also reviewed. Two anesthesiologists have summarized their observations and their inferences as follows:

Of the 191 cases reviewed, 136 (71%) involved general anesthesia and 55 (29%) regional anesthesia. Unfortunately, we have no way to determine the total number of anesthetic episodes which occurred over the 11-year period (the denominator), and thus we cannot project any specific incidence figures. While it is obviously low, we decided to go ahead and analyze the cases by the type of anesthesia employed.

Deficits in patient monitoring were found underlying 18 problems of the 136 total occurring during general anesthesia; in three instances of general anesthesia, the anesthesiologist wasn't in the room at the time of the disaster. Three quite clear-cut cases of 'altered' records were also identified; in one instance, three obviously different anesthesiologic records were identified for a single patient! Cases of the wrong drug, the wrong blood, and even the wrong patient also occurred. While we have no way of knowing whether any comparable 'errors' went unrecognized elsewhere during the 11-year period, we suspect they did. Fail-safe 'monitoring' to avoid such possibilities would seem to be mandatory.

Also among the general anesthetic episodes, severe airway problems occurred, with eight difficult intubations leading to four deaths and four damaged brains; there were seven erroneous esophogeal intubations and others with mucous plugs, bronchial spasms, etc., all leading to claims. Damage to teeth accounted for approximately 20% of the claims and settlements; removal of oral airways and their replacement by nasal airways during trips to recovery rooms may curtail such episodes. Peripheral nerve injury served as a basis for 10% of these general anesthesia related claims—the ulnar nerve being the most commonly involved. Isolated instances of hepatitis related to halothane, six cases of air embolism occurring during the cardiopulmonary bypass, and four occurring during 'sitting craniotomies,' plus instances of ventricular fibrillation round out the other obvious detected causes—and give hints at the preventive measures which may be possible.

In contrast for the 55 instances of *regional* anesthesia, 14 involved cardiac arrests with either brain damage or death; 16 involved permanent peripheral nerve damage; and 7 were associated with seizures. In terms of etiology, we found no difficulty in judging that inept administration or maintenance of the anesthesia was clearly responsible for 14 of the 55 cases.

When we analyzed the type of regional anesthesia involved, spinal anesthesia was associated with 10 of the 14 cardiac arrests; it was also implicated in nerve injuries to nine patients but—as has been previously reported extensively—could not have been anatomically the explanation for the majority. Lumbar epidural block was associated with three life-threatening complications; caudal epidural block with five, and brachial plexus block with one. Again, for each area, peripheral nerve problems were not easily explainable by the anatomy involved.

When we attempted to look at the specific anesthetic agent used, we were unable to detect any specific associations. When we looked at the performance of the anesthesia as its documentation could be compared to community standards, we were astounded to determine that—among the general anesthetic episodes where we concluded the documented performance was above community standards—50% still resulted in plaintiff verdicts. When regional anesthesia was comparably appraised, 80% resulted in plaintiff verdicts!

To us, even more devastating was our determination that at least three of the involved anesthesiologists successfully suicided in the period immediately following a malpractice episode. We would strongly urge that some type of counseling be made available to such individuals to help them during that trying period. We also determined that seven patients who had received rapid intravenous administration of antibiotics during the anesthetic episode underwent cardiovascular collapse, with five subsequent deaths. Moreover in three instances, rapid onset cardiac arrests occurred during the use of hypobaric anesthesia for obese patients. Avoidance measures seemed available in both situations.

All in all, our specialty society has the opportunity—with data such as have been gathered—to institute extensive changes by our members as it pursues its mission. Quite clearly, such changes can do much to make anesthesia care far better for patients on the one hand and to avoid malpractice problems on the other. Admittedly, we're still not able to explain or prevent some of the problems, but for many we do have a clear course of action waiting to be implemented.

Richard Solozzi, M.D.
Richard Ward, M.D.

What You Can Do

In your hospital, does your medical staff or medical executive committee conduct a careful review of untoward incidents involving physicians to try to impose preventive measures? Does the anesthesiologist ever leave the operating room so the patient is in fact unattended? Are you sure? In your hospital, have fail-safe monitoring mechanisms been introduced to assure that proper patient, proper extremity, proper blood identification all occur? Do they work?

Quite clearly, the specialty of Anesthesiology deserves congratulations from the rest of the profession for the job they've done in the state of Washington. Other specialties will benefit greatly from replicating their efforts.

SECTION 40

The Limits of Confidentiality

Case. C. P., a 32-year-old always-healthy individual, sued the state of Washington after being injured in a two-automobile accident. The other driver, L. K., on probation from a burglary conviction, had been traveling at an estimated 50–60 miles per hour and ran a red light before striking C. P.'s car. Witnesses concluded that L. K. was under the influence of drugs. Five days before the accident, L. K. had been released from Western State Hospital, where he had been receiving psychiatric care.

Apparently one month earlier L. K. had been found in his blood-soaked bed by his brother, after he "had taken a knife to himself and cut out his left testicle." Taken to a hospital, he was found to be delusional with hallucinations resulting from a renewed problem with drugs (Phencyclidine). Subsequently, L. K. was involuntarily committed to Western State Hospital for not more than 72 hours under the care of Dr. A. M.

Dr. M. learned of the burglary probation, but not of the terms. He went on to make a diagnosis of "schizophrenic reaction," due primarily to Phencyclidine, and he prescribed Navane. L. K.'s commitment was extended so that treatment could be continued for an additional 14 days. Then he was discharged, even though the night before his release he had been found driving his car recklessly in circles on hospital grounds, having just returned on a pass. Five days later, the automobile accident occurred.

Ms. C. P.'s action was based on the premise that the state and its employee physician, Dr. A. M., were negligent in failing to protect her from a dangerous individual. She held that the doctor had failed to seek additional confinement or report the parole violation. The jury agreed, and an appeal to the Washington State Supreme Court later sustained the verdict.

Discussion

While the state raised at least seven different issues in its appeal, physicians and other health professionals will want to take particular note of this one: "Does the physician's (psychotherapist's) duty to protect the safety of others override his obligation to the patient per se?" Apparently, under common law, no such duty is held to exist. But a number of our nation's courts have now recognized an exception that establishes such a duty when a special relationship exists between the defendant (the physician or psychotherapist) and potential victims of a patient's action. The Washington State Supreme Court once concluded that a physician prescribing a drug with known side effects of somnolence, who failed to warn the patient of this side effect, was liable for injuries suffered by others after a patient so treated fell asleep and caused a bus accident. The court in its deliberations cited the landmark *Tarasoff* case in which a University of California psychotherapist failed to inform a potential victim that a patient under treatment had threatened murder. The psychotherapist was found guilty of negligence—after the murder took place. A California court concluded that the psychotherapist did have a duty to warn the person threatened (or the police) when he determined, or should have determined, that "serious danger of violence to another" existed.

Other decisions have concurred with the finding in the California case, sustaining the overall conclusion that a duty does exist to recognize that a "potential for severe danger exists," and that the recognition ought to be acted upon expeditiously. In Dr. A. M.'s case, he was of the opinion that the patient would not have been dangerous had he remained free of additional Phencyclidine and had he consumed the prescribed Navane. Unfortunately, the patient failed on both counts.

The issue of "privileged (confidential) communication" in Washington State appears to be a bit more complex. The court concluded that Dr. A. M. was, in fact, prohibited from reporting the involuntary commitment to the probation officer at the time of the incident, or even commenting on it to the trial court judge at the time of the trial. Thus, the distinction would seem to be that the recognition and reporting of danger is required of the physician, but that reporting such dangers to officials of the law may not be acceptable if there is any violation of the current Involuntary Commitment Act.

The implications of this case for psychotherapists and physicians are obvious. Each is expected to observe confidentiality of communication—up to a point—where clear and present danger is believed to exist. Then, at that point, a warning must be given to the potential victim or to the police. From a societal point of view, it makes sense. But from the vantage point of the "disturbed patient," however, this may not hold true. What obligation does the physician have to inform the patient that such a report is to be given?

Lest the situation seem entirely theoretical, consider a recent case in California where a marriage counselor reported the sexual abuse of a 12-year-old female by her stepfather—a fact which was readily admitted to the marriage counselor by the family at the time of their self-referral for therapy. The case gained national notoriety when, at a subsequent trial, the girl refused to testify against her stepfather and was jailed for eight days as a consequence. In light of that publicity, are troubled families more or less likely to seek help?

What You Can Do

In your individual practice, is this or an associated type of problem, likely to occur? Should it happen, how would you act? Where can you turn for help? At your hospital, has the issue ever been discussed among physicians?

SECTION 41

Claims Review Issues

Case 1. T. K., a 37-year-old woman, sought a tubal ligation, and arrangements were made to use a laparoscopic approach under general anesthesia. Unfortunately, during the procedure, she developed bradycardia and hypotension, followed almost immediately by a cardiac arrest that lasted six minutes. She was resuscitated but suffered severe brain damage.

When her case was reviewed by the Claims Review Panel and its consultants, it was determined that (1) there was no documentation of an informed consent relating to the general anesthesia; (2) documentation of proper patient monitoring was missing: no precordial or esophageal stethoscope was used and there was no documentation of continuous monitoring of the peripheral pulse; (3) despite the patient's long history of occupational lung disease (for which she had been receiving industrial insurance benefits for approximately one year), there was no such documentation anywhere in her medical records, nor had the fact been known preoperatively by the anesthesiologist involved; and (4) following the cardiac arrest, the anesthesiologist failed to use any airway device. Instead he relied on manual bagging with 100 percent oxygen, and at no time was the patient ever placed on a cardiac monitor after the arrest.

As a consequence of these points, the Claims Review Panel concluded that probable negligence existed and that it caused the patient's impairment. The panel recommended seeking a compromise with the plaintiff's representatives; a six-figure indemnity payment concluded the case.

Case 2. M. B., a 52-year-old male previously always apparently well, had recurring episodes of chest pain for approximately one week. One evening he developed an "attack" which was accompanied by apprehension and diaphoresis. Shortly thereafter, he collapsed. A medic unit was called and upon arrival allegedly found the patient momentarily pulseless, but he resumed his heartbeat without CPR. He was transferred by ambulance to an emergency room, where he was examined and had a twelve-lead EKG performed. The EKG was interpreted as normal, and shortly thereafter he was permitted to go home—only to return to the emergency room DOA a few hours later. At post-mortem, a fresh thrombus was found that occluded 90 percent of the proximal left anterior descending coronary artery. Atherosclerosis severely compromised the circumflex coronary artery and evidence of old infarcts was widespread.

A Claims Review Panel—composed of peer physicians selected by WSMA and consultants—was severely critical of the emergency room personnel who permitted the patient to return home. An overwhelming majority of the panel believed that admission and observation had been called for and that a serious error in judgment had occurred. Again, a recommendation for compromise was made and a large payment followed.

Case 3. A. T., a 32-year-old male, had a long history of relapsing back pain most recently accompanied by weakness in the left leg. He was seen by an orthopedist, who diagnosed a herniated disc and subsequently performed surgery. For six months postoperatively, the patient's symptoms apparently subsided, only to recur. After a repeat diagnostic imaging, a second disc procedure was carried out. It resulted in minimal if any improvement in the patient's symptoms, and he also purportedly developed impotence. As this case was reviewed by a Claims Review Panel and its consultants, it became apparent that both surgical procedures had, in fact, been carried out quite properly, but unfortunately on the wrong disc. Needless to say, the Review Panel could not recommend an ardent defense.

Discussion

A recently completed report and analysis of 711 claims closed un-der the WSMA sponsored liability insurance program during 1976 to 1980, shows that Claims Review panels reviewed 118 (16.6%) of the claims prior to their closures. These panels, consisting of a chairman and seven to ten representative peer physicians, are appointed by WSMA. They are convened on call of the carrier, the involved phy-sician, or by WSMA to advise the carrier, the defense attorney, and the defendant physician of their in-depth analysis of the case at hand and of their opinion on whether the claim should be defended or settled, or a compromise should be sought. All conclusions, delib-erations, opinions, and other findings are the "work product" of the defense attorney, are privileged for his or her use only, and thus are not subject to subpoena.

Members of the panels serve voluntarily, contributing significantly to the better management of the disputes at hand. While their work is a time-consuming and often onerous task, all panel members gain significant insights into malpractice problems. Under the expanded Claims Review Panel Program, WSMA physicians and multiple car-riers will retain this service as a catalyst for most logical resolutions of malpractice problems, i.e., better defense, more aggressive claims management, etc. At the same time, members of the panels meet with their county medical societies and their hospital medical staffs to share their experiences (naturally maintaining appropriate con-fidentiality) and to make recommendations about how individual physicians and hospital medical staffs can avoid allegations of neg-ligence in the future.

The 118 claims submitted to the Claims Review panels eventually accounted for 62.4 percent of the total indemnity dollars paid to plaintiffs. Thus, the selection of cases has been appropriate for re-view by the panels; it has focused successfully on significant issues.

One conclusion is unanimous among those physicians who have served on the panels for any prolonged period of time: a significant percentage of the cases brought before them do, in fact, contain sub-stantial evidence of probable negligence, which has served as the ba-sis for the settlement. Attesting to this inference of negligence is the further finding that in 98 of the 118 claims where precise information exists, 51 (52%) were recommended for settlement, 24 (24%) for compromise, and 23 (23%) for defense, suggesting that "negligence" is, in fact, a significant problem for all of us.

Supporting evidence in the medical literature goes back to the mid-1960s when Schimmel analyzed a large series of hospital admissions and determined by subjecting the records to critical review that it was possible to identify significant instances of what we would today call "probable negligence." Moreover, a March 1981 article in the *New England Journal of Medicine* (304:628–42) attested to the same point of view: 36 percent of 815 patients had iatrogenic illness. In a 1981 review of 711 closed claims by malpractice experts, it appeared that some 65.6 percent involved negligence, and that for 250 claims it was a moderate to high degree of negligence.

Obviously, proposed resolutions to the malpractice problem must take the negligence factor into account. While there is no consensus by Claims Review Panel members on how best to avoid repetition of such performances, the panel members have been unanimous in urging that efforts at redress take place. As noted, "attempts at tort reform or manipulating the insurability of physicians simply is inadequate. Neither the revision of tort law, insurance underwriting practices, nor insurance company claims management of professional liability cases can be expected to impact positively to any large degree upon the present national medical malpractice scene."

What You Can Do

In your hospital, does a mechanism exist—and is it used—to detect and review incidents possibly threatening to patients? Does a mechanism exist for patients to let you know how they feel they have been treated? Does your medical records department conduct "generic screening" of all discharge records seeking out possible malpractice patterns?

13

Looking Ahead

Each of the foregoing chapters has attempted to highlight one or more contributors to the 1980's medical malpractice scene. The focus has been on those issues perceived by the author as able to be influenced by changes in physicians' individual or collective behavior. Some experts maintain that as many as two-thirds of today's cases stem from administrative or managerial shortcomings as opposed to problems of knowledge or judgment; apparently we know what to do—it just does not get done. Many changes aimed at overcoming those shortcomings have already been specified; still others are self evident, and some are yet to be recognized. Suffice it to note, however, that were all possible changes in physicians' behavior achieved, a malpractice problem would probably persist—given the differing perceptions of medical care by the public, their advocates, the mass media, our legislators, and our courts, as well as physicians themselves. Given a perfect hospital or office environment—even if random accidents did not occur—there would be some less than ideal medical care outcomes.

Injured patients, on their own or encouraged by others, eventually (and understandably) take recourse in our courts and our jury system. What with continuing inflation of health care costs on the one hand, and our burgeoning health care technology and its associated likelihood of error on the other, allegations of medical malpractice can become a social device to shift costs, to secure "justice," to punish wrongdoers, or to implement the Robin Hood principle of economics. Allegations of this kind are most unlikely to disappear. Thus, I feel certain that the frequency and severity of malpractice cases are

likely to continue to escalate unless some massive socioeconomic solution is created. My crystal ball indicates the result may simply be
an altered name for the problem.

In truth, this predictable series of events jeopardizes the effectiveness of our health care system. It undermines the confidence of patients in their physicians. Its adversarial component shakes the confidence of physicians in their patients. And everybody worries about
going to the hospital. All parties are on the defensive. As much as
$40 billion is thought to be expended annually for "defensive med-
icine," undertaken to avoid allegations of medical malpractice. The
cost of such defensive medicine far exceeds the cost of the malpractice insurance itself. Moreover, such defensive behavior on the part
of the patient inhibits him/her from accepting any of the depen-
dence or lack of complete autonomy that hospitalization sometimes
makes necessary. The resultant troubled relationships can prove detrimental to both the patient and the system.

A number of alternative solutions to this turmoil have been proposed. Thus, the use of arbitration processes, adjudicating panels of
experts, or other nonjury systems to resolve disputes; the adoption
of a "workman's compensation modality"; reliance on a no-fault alternative; and the imposition of a dollar "cap" on awards are a few
examples proposed to replace the current costly mechanism. In virtually all states, resolving malpractice allegations continues to impose
a considerable burden on our already overtaxed judicial system. There
are some few who propose having the government assume total responsibility and financial accountability—but such proposals have little likelihood of adoption as things now stand.

Certainly, as Curran has noted in the *NEJM*, the massive legislative
efforts of 1975 to bring about a legislative solution to the malpractice
crisis failed to affect either the *frequency* or the *severity* of awards, save
in those states which enacted a monetary ceiling on awards. Moreover, among those states at least four have now seen their State Supreme Courts declare the ceiling unconstitutional, while several others (e.g., Florida and Indiana) have seen their initial respite come to
an end as inflation and escalation in awards threaten their excess
award funds.

Other states have championed the formation of self-insurance programs by physicians. Collectively, the programs have formed the
Physicians Insurance Association of America (PIAA) to pool their re-

sources and experiences in coping with the crisis. After an initial honeymoon period of economic well-being, their losses have now begun to drive up premiums so that they closely parallel private commercial carriers' premiums. Certainly the physician-sponsored companies can and should be somewhat more efficient and effective than their commercial counterparts, but the savings are unlikely to be all that extensive, unless severe underwriting limitations are imposed. Their biggest benefit will be at long last to arrange for the compilation of reliable epidemiologic data—but even the PIAA has been reluctant to embark on such studies.

Other states look to the courts as a potential mechanism to turn around the problem. Little doubt exists, for example, that for our Canadian counterparts, the courts have in fact been instrumental in curtailing the mushrooming of malpractice awards. There, for example, 1982 saw physicians pay a standard premium of approximately $350 yearly versus the over-$5,000 that is paid by the average insured physician in the United States. Interestingly, the Canadian program has undergone recent change so as to reflect the variable risk of different classes of physicians via differential premiums, which might be predicted to affect malpractice settlements. In Canada the Bar frowns on (or in some cases has outlawed) the contingency-fee system; a judge and not a jury decides the case and the judge on his or her own specifies the damages; moreover, punitive damages are most rare. Facts as opposed to emotions dominate resolution of the dispute.

In contrast, the courts of the United States can hardly be seen as impeding the explosion of the negligence actions seen. To the contrary, they have led the way in espousing new legal doctrines (informed consent, wrongful birth, wrongful life, etc.) and discarding old ones (charitable immunity), all of which serve to increase rather than decrease the potential for expensive resolution of negligence actions. Philosophically, however, few can really challenge the basis for the courts' actions. In fact, many of their changes seem long overdue. Nonetheless, the courts cannot be expected to subdue the tempest of the malpractice problem.

If not to the legislature, if not to the insurance mechanism, if not to the courts, where are physicians in particular and society in general to turn for solutions of the problem?

Although each proposal has its attractions and its advocates, many people feel that an essential component of any overall solution would include an incentive-driven provider (physician). Such incentives should (1) keep down that provider's own costs and losses; (2) avoid tarnishing the provider's professional reputation and image; (3) assure a sense of more rather than less professional satisfaction from the individual provider's work, and (4) avoid encouraging the provider to seek excessive diagnostic or therapeutic endeavors. And obviously that provider's patients must be assured of quality work.

Agreeing with this postulate, it has been my goal to try to adapt the medical model of disease elimination to the malpractice scene. Here the first step is to uncover and refine the epidemiology of the problem; the second is to pinpoint the multiple causes of the problem and to quantify the respective size of each contributor; and the third is to develop and then implement preventive mechanisms rather than simply seeking out therapeutic nostrums. WSMA has taken such an approach to medical malpractice in the state of Washington. Its "Risk Management Program" aims to define the epidemiology, pinpoint causal factors, eliminate etiologic factors, and introduce improvements into systems management, as well as into individual physician behavior. The goal: eliminate the causes of malpractice, instead of simply relying on tort reform measures and altered insurance mechanisms to overcome the problem. Unless the medical profession and its individual members continue to assume active roles in addressing this issue, the problem of malpractice allegations can only grow to disastrous proportions. With the profession's participation— acting on facts as opposed to rumor—the possibility of avoiding such disaster is within our grasp.

References Cited

Anderson, R. M., G. V. Fleming, and C. A. Aday. 1981. "The Public View as Input for Medical Manpower Training." In *Socioeconomic Issues of Health*, ed. Musacchio and Hough. Chicago: AMA, 1981.

Brent, R. I. 1982. "The Irresponsible Expert Witness." *Pediatrics* 70:754–62.

Bryant, G. D., and G. R. Norman. 1980. "Expressions of Probability: Words and Numbers." *New England Journal of Medicine* 302:411.

Chapman, C. B. 1982. "Stratton vs. Swanland: The Fourteenth-Century Ancestor of the Law of Malpractice." *Pharos* 45:20–24.

Curran, W. J. 1983. Law-Medicine Notes. "Medical Malpractice Claims since the Crisis of 1975: Some Good News and Some Bad." *New England Journal of Medicine* 309:1107–9.

Curran, W. J., and E. D. Shapiro. 1982. *Law, Medicine and Forensic Science*. Boston: Little, Brown.

Department of Health, Education and Welfare. 1973. *Report of the Secretary's Commission on Medical Malpractice*. Washington, D.C.: Government Printing Office.

Finamore, E. P. 1983. "Jefferson v. Griffin Spaulding County Hospital Authority: Court-Ordered Surgery to Protect the Life of an Unborn Child." *American Journal of Law and Medicine* 9:83–101.

Frey, E. F. 1982. "Medicolegal History: A Review of Significant Publications and Educational Developments. *Law, Medicine and Health* 10:56–60.

Goldsmith, D., and W. O. Robertson. 1980. "Medical Discipline—A New Direction." *DEA/Registrant* 6:4–7.

Hilfiker, D. T. 1983. "Facing Our Ethical Choices." *New England Journal of Medicine* 308:716–19.

Lundberg, G. D. 1984. "Expert Witness for Whom?" *Journal of the American Medical Association* 252:251.

Meadow, R. 1982. "Munchhausen's Syndrome by Proxy." *Arch. Dis. Child* 57:92–98.

Richards, E. P., and K. C. Rathbun. 1983. *Medical Risk Management*. Rockville, Md: Aspen Systems Corp.

173

Robertson, W. O. 1971. "Professional Liability Insurance Protection: An Affirmative Action Program." *Journal of Medical Education* 46:858–62.

———. 1976. "The Rights of Doctors." *Bioethics Northwest* 1:6–7.

———. 1981. "Hand Washing in Hospitals." *New England Journal of Medicine* 305:963.

———. 1983. "Quantifying the Meaning of Words." *Journal of the American Medical Association* 249:2631–32.

Rosoff, A. J. 1981. *Informed Consent*. Rockville, Md.: Aspen Publications.

Tso, Y., and W. O. Robertson. 1980. "Illegibility of Prescriptions: Some Worrisome Implications." *Veterinary and Human Toxicology* 22:10–12.

U.S. Senate Committee on Government Operations. 1969. *Medical Malpractice: The Patient vs. the Physician*. Washington, D.C.: Government Printing Office.

Appendix

Risk Management Review Units

As Washington malpractice experiences have been reviewed and then compared with national data compiled by the National Association of Insurance Commissioners and others, it has been possible to identify a number of causative factors which seem susceptible to either change or elimination at the level of the individual hospital's medical staff or on the part of the individual physician. To assist those physicians and their committees, a series of thirty "Risk Management Review Units" (i.e., audit programs) have been developed and circulated to all the chiefs of staff and hospital administrators across the state. Implementation is recommended via each hospital's "Quality Assurance Program." The format identifies the issue, provides an "outcome goal" (or objective) and then offers a relatively simple approach to data-gathering retrospectively or prospectively via chart review, observations, or simple surveys. Obviously, each hospital can enrich the specific approach if warranted. Outcomes are shared appropriately and action then follows.

Two follow-up surveys have found a surprising amount of risk management activity at the level of the individual hospital; almost all hospitals had employed the review units. Most respondents were ready and willing to put in the time and effort to participate in the Risk Management Program. Although initially no effort was made to collect data from all participating hospitals in a central location, individual hospital results have been submitted, reported back to the WSMA, to other hospitals, and to specialty societies, confirming improvement in virtually all of the topics at issue. The Washington State Professional Standards Review Organization (WSPSRO) and the Washington Professional Review Organization have accepted these efforts as fulfilling their (and the JCAH's) requirements for the Quality Assurance Program. Review units are prepared as necessary to respond to new problems.

175

Topic 1

Head Injury Monitoring

Issue. Failure to order specific monitoring procedures for patients admitted to hospitals with head injuries

Solution. Assure for all patients admitted with a diagnosis of head injury (and/or discharged with such diagnosis) that the order sheet contains a specific order re: monitoring of vital signs, and that the "patient care data sheets" (progress notes, nurses' notes, ICU data forms) confirm that the monitoring orders were, in fact, carried out.

Review Procedure

1. Obtain a sample of 30 charts of patients discharged with a diagnosis of head injury (or all charts of such patients discharged over the last three years).

2. Review the order sheet on each chart for the presence of specific monitoring orders re: temperature, pulse, respiration, blood pressure, and observations of level of consciousness.

3. Review the nurses' notes, progress notes, or any intensive care flow sheet for the presence of documentation indicating compliance with the orders.

4. Isolate and itemize any deficits detected.

Actions To Be Taken

1. If all is in order, so notify the Medical Executive Committee and the medical staff at the next staff meeting.

2. If problems exist, devise a solution, implement it, re-audit the issue, and report to the Medical Executive Committee and the medical staff about that activity.

Added Point of Emphasis. In some hospitals, a preprinted head injury monitoring procedure has been approved for use by the medical staff, obviating some of the problems which occur.

Topic 2

Emergency Room Discharges

Issue. Failure to document instructions being given to patients dismissed from the emergency room

Solution. 100 percent of ER charts should have appropriate discharge directions—and in legible form.

Review Procedure

1. Obtain a sample of 50 charts of patients recently managed in your emergency room.

2. Examine each chart for discharge directions, to include: (a) treatment measures, if any; (b) activity limitations, if any; (c) drugs prescribed, if any; (d) location of scheduled follow-up, if any; (e) time of scheduled follow-up, if any.

Actions To Be Taken

1. If all is in order, so notify the Medical Executive Committee and the medical staff at the next staff meeting.

2. If problems exist, devise a solution, implement it, re-audit the issue, and report to the Medical Executive Committee and the medical staff about that activity.

Added Point of Emphasis. In many hospitals, the emergency room physician and charge nurse review all charts daily before they are sent from the emergency room for billing or filing.

Topic 3

Drug Usage Review

Issue.   Erroneous prescriptions for drug dosages ordered in hospitals

Solution.   Assure that, in the absence of a specific order to the contrary, all drug dosage is carried out in accordance with drug dosage schedules provided in the Physician's Desk Reference (or your preferred standard). (The issue of indications will be dealt with later.)

Review Procedure
1. Obtain a sample of 30 charts of recently discharged patients.
2. Prepare a list from each chart of up to, but no more than, five drugs per individual as prescribed in each chart, the amount to be given, and the frequency of administration ordered.
3. Obtain a copy of the PDR (or your chosen standard) and arrange that a physician and pharmacist compare the orders as specified with the limitations recommended in the PDR, isolating and identifying any differences obtained.

Actions To Be Taken
1. If all is in order, so notify the Medical Executive Committee and the medical staff at the next staff meeting.
2. If problems exist, devise a solution, implement it, re-audit the issue, and report to the Medical Executive Committee and the medical staff about that activity.

Added Point of Emphasis.   In some hospitals, particularly those with "unit dose systems," the pharmacy monitors drug dosage carefully and is authorized to limit the distribution of drugs when they are ordered in dosages outside of recommended limits.

Topic 4

Informed Consent

Issue.   Failure to document an "informed consent" in instances of surgical procedures conducted in hospitals

Solution.   100 percent of all charts of patients who undergo surgical procedures in Washington hospitals should include an informed consent document.

Review Procedure
1. Obtain a sample of 50 charts of patients who recently underwent surgical procedures at your hospital.
2. Review each for the presence or absence of *documented* informed consent.

Actions To Be Taken
1. If all is in order, so notify the Medical Executive Committee and the medical staff at the next staff meeting.
2. If problems exist, devise a solution, implement it, re-audit the issue within a given time, and report to the Medical Executive Committee and the medical staff about that activity.

Added Point of Emphasis.   In many hospitals, the operating room supervisor or the anesthesiologist enforces the requirement of documenting informed consent—no documentation equals no anesthesia!

Topic 5

Staff Bylaws Procedures

Issue.   Failure of medical staffs to have clearly specified procedures guaranteeing due process for individuals being terminated from that medical staff—either physicians or physician administrators (president of medical staff)

Solution.   Assure that 100 percent of the hospitals' bylaws do, in fact, contain adequate procedural guarantees of due process regarding the dismissal of a physician from the medical staff or of an officer from the medical staff organization.

Review Procedure.   Obtain a copy of the current (most recent) Medical Staff Bylaws and analyze for the presence of: (1) due process guarantees regarding the dismissal of a physician from the medical staff; (2) due process guarantees regarding the termination of an officer from the medical staff organization.

Actions To Be Taken
1. If all is in order, so notify the Medical Executive Committee and the medical staff at the next staff meeting.
2. If problems exist, devise a solution, implement it, re-audit the issue, and report to the Medical Executive Committee and the medical staff about that activity.

Added Point of Emphasis.   The 1980s are seeing the Joint Commission on Accreditation of Hospitals pay particular attention to this item, which fits in well with concerns voiced by WSMA, WSHA, and individual practitioners, as well as trial attorneys.

Topic 6

No Code Procedures

Issue. "No code" procedures

Solution. Assure that 100 percent of the medical staffs in the state have documented in the records of that staff organization that "no code" procedures have been considered and that a policy has been adopted which provides guidelines for the conduct of such choices.

Review Procedure. Obtain the minutes of the Medical Executive Committee and/or of the medical staff over the last two years and review them for the existence of: (1) documentation that the issue of "no code" has been discussed; (2) documentation that a policy had been recommended with guidelines to be followed in the hospital regarding no code activities; (3) distribution of the policy and guidelines to all members of the medical staff and nursing staff.

Actions To Be Taken
1. If all is in order, so notify the Medical Executive Committee and the medical staff at the next staff meeting.
2. If problems exist, devise a solution, implement it, re-audit the issue, and report to the Medical Executive Committee and the medical staff about that activity.

Added Point of Emphasis. Over the past year in Washington State, the medical association has been wrestling with the appropriate guidelines to respond to requests from the Washington State Nurses Association that the "rules of the road" be clarified; these guidelines have now been distributed widely across the state.

Topic 7

Use of Rh-Immune Globulin in Abortions

Issue. Failure to administer Rh-immune globulin to patients undergoing "terminations of pregnancy"

Solution. Assure that all hospitals have procedures to insure that all patients undergoing terminations of pregnancy are managed appropriately for the possible use of Rh-immune globulin.

Review Procedure
1. Obtain a sample of 50 charts of patients undergoing recent termination of pregnancy in your hospital.
2. Review each chart for the presence or absence of blood typing (A, B, and O, as well as Rh).
3. In all instances of non-typed individuals and those who were typed Rh negative (with some clarifying information about the absence of sensitization) look for evidence in the order sheet that Rh-immune globulin had, in fact, been ordered and administered; or, look in the progress notes and/or drug administration sheets for evidence of same.

Actions To Be Taken
1. If all is in order, so notify the Medical Executive Committee and the medical staff at the next staff meeting.
2. If problems exist, devise a solution, implement it, re-audit the issue, and report to the Medical Executive Committee and the medical staff about that activity.

Added Point of Emphasis. According to a statewide survey done in 1980, somewhat less than 75 percent of patients judged to benefit from use of Rh-immune globulin in these situations were, in fact, receiving it—in contrast to better than 95 percent of patients delivering at term. As an explanation for current Rh-hemolytic disease, inadequate management of termination procedures stands out.

Topic 8

Operative Reports

Issue. Failure to dictate or transcribe an operative report in a timely fashion (e.g., in one to two weeks) and have it signed and entered into the patient's medical record

Solution. 100 percent of all charts of patients who undergo surgical procedures should have a completed and signed operative report in the patient's chart within 7 to 14 days.

Review Procedure

1. With the cooperation and commitment of your quality assurance coordinator and your Medical Records Department, locate and review for each day of the week (Monday through Friday) 10 postoperative surgical patients' charts, on the seventh postoperative day.

2. Analyze each chart for the presence or absence of a signed operative report.

Actions To Be Taken

1. If all is in order, so notify the Medical Executive Committee and the medical staff at the next staff meeting.

2. If problems exist, devise a solution, implement it, re-audit the issue, and report to the Medical Executive Committee and the medical staff about that activity.

Added Point of Emphasis. In Colorado, two different judges have ruled and so instructed the juries that when the operative report had not been dictated and entered into the chart within 30 days, the jury was to ignore it totally as a possible basis of defense.

TOPIC 9

Emergency C-Sections

Issue.   Unexplained delays in initiating emergency Cesarean sections

Solution.   All hospitals in which deliveries are carried out should evolve plans and procedures to be able to initiate an emergency Cesarean section in less than 15 minutes.

Review Procedure
1. With the cooperation of the Obstetrics, Anesthesiology, and Medical Records departments, identify 20 instances occurring over the last year wherein an emergency C-section was called for. Review each chart to determine the time lapse between the decision to proceed to C-section and the initiation of the procedure.
2. Take the mean time lapse and compare it with the sought-for standard.

Actions To Be Taken
1. If all is in order, so notify the Medical Executive Committee and the medical staff at the next staff meeting.
2. If problems exist, devise a solution, implement it, re-audit the issue, and report to the Medical Executive Committee and the medical staff about that activity.

Added Point of Emphasis.   In a number of Washington hospitals, plans and procedures have been developed; some are reported actually to conduct mock trials.

Topic 10

X-Ray Reports to the Charts

Issue.   Tardy arrival of X-ray reports to the medical chart

Solution.   100 percent of all x-ray reports should be dictated, transcribed, and entered in the chart within 18 to 24 hours—including emergency X-rays taken on the weekend.

Review Procedure

1. With the cooperation of your Radiology Department, itemize the names of patients having x-rays taken on various days of the week.

2. With the cooperation of your Medical Records Department, review each chart identified from step 1 approximately 24 hours later for the presence or absence of the x-ray report.

3. Assure that some of the assessments are made for reports taken in the emergency room or on the floors over the weekend.

Actions To Be Taken

1. If all is in order, so notify the Medical Executive Committee and the medical staff at the next staff meeting.

2. If problems exist, devise a solution, implement it, re-audit the issue, and report to the Medical Executive Committee and the medical staff about that activity.

Added Point of Emphasis.   To assure that your Radiology Department doesn't become paranoid, use the same approach in assessing timeliness of other reports appearing on the charts—EKG's, EEG's, microbiology, etc. Some hospitals have instituted "fail safe" back-up mechanisms via computer terminals for "electronic mail."

Topic 11

Incident Reports

Issue.   Failure to notify the appropriate insurance carrier in a timely manner regarding a potential negligence action

Solution.   Reports filed by physicians, nurses and/or other hospital staff employees of incidents which may result in an allegation of malpractice against medical staff members should be discussed by the hospital administration with either the individual involved or the leadership of the medical staff. To assure such a process, a policy and procedure approved by the hospital administration, the medical staff, and the hospital's Board of Trustees should be documented.

Review Procedure
1. Obtain the cooperation of your hospital administrator to review with him or her the policies and procedures being implemented by the hospital to deal with "incident reports" prepared by hospital staff.
2. If the above fails to involve the attending physician or the leadership of the medical staff, prepare a simple procedure with the cooperation of hospital administration to assure amelioration of the problem.

Actions To Be Taken
1. If all is in order, so notify the Medical Executive Committee and the medical staff at the next staff meeting.
2. If problems exist, devise a solution, implement it, re-audit the issue, and report to the Medical Executive Committee and the medical staff about that activity.

Added Point of Emphasis.   While "jousting" between and among physicians presents a significant problem to the profession, interprofessional jousting also contributes its fair share of problems. Open communication regarding "untoward incidents" between (or among) the parties involved serves to avoid some subsequent dilemmas. Incident reports which have actually existed in hospitals would have gone a long way toward avoiding liability had they been known to the physician's carrier.

Topic 12

Multiple M.D.s Writing Orders

Issue.   Conflicting, competing, and incompatible drug orders written by multiple physicians for a single patient. As many as nine different physicians have been involved in writing orders for one patient during a single 24-hour period!

Solution.   Minimize—not necessarily eliminate—multiple authorship of orders in medical records.

Review Procedure

1. Obtain a sample of 50 charts of recently discharged patients, preferably including at least 10 patients who have been in the intensive care or coronary care units.

2. Review the order sheets—no more than three pages per chart—for the total number of attending physicians (or other physicians) writing orders, as well as the total number of orders written.

3. Tally both the mean (average) number of physician authors per chart and the total number of orders per chart, then calculate the number of orders per physician.

4. Review all charts for potential conflicting orders where more than three authors contributed, or the average number of orders per physician is less than five.

Actions To Be Taken

1. If all is in order, so notify the Medical Executive Committee and the medical staff at the next staff meeting.

2. If problems exist in your hospital, consider potential solutions and discuss them with your staff and with the Medical Executive Committee. Upon achieving a consensus, attempt to publicize the solution and implement it; re-audit the issue and report back to the Medical Executive Committee and the medical staff in the future.

Added Point of Emphasis.   In some hospitals, all consultants are precluded from writing orders directly; they enter recommendations into the progress notes for the attending physician to accept or reject and write appropriate orders himself/herself, or they communicate with that attending physician by phone or in person.

Topic 13

Abbreviations in Medical Records

Issue. Erroneous interpretations of abbreviations in medical records by physicians, nurses, pharmacists, and others who use the records

Solution. Minimize the use of any abbreviations (or acronyms) in medical records—even though each hospital (in order to comply with the accrediting agency's requirements) has a listing of "approved abbreviations" to be used in its medical records.

Review Procedure

1. Obtain a sample of 30 records of patients recently discharged from the hospital.

2. Select one page of progress notes and one page of order sheets from each record and identify the abbreviations or acronyms used on each page.

3. Tally all abbreviations from the progress notes on one sheet and from the order sheet on another.

4. Compare all entries on each sheet with the hospital's approved abbreviation list—again, tallying all agreements as well as all non-agreements.

5. Divide all resulting numbers by sample size (n = 30) to obtain derivative rates, i.e., unapproved abbreviations per chart.

Actions To Be Taken

1. If all is in order (i.e., no abbreviations or acronyms are used), so notify the Medical Executive Committee and the medical staff at the next meeting. If only approved abbreviations are used, emphasize that point.

2. If problems exist, discuss how to achieve some type of resolution to minimize the use of abbreviations, implement the proposed solution, re-audit the issue after six months, and report to the Medical Executive Committee and the medical staff about your activity and your results.

Added Point of Emphasis.   At one of Washington State's hospitals, a random sample of approved abbreviations was distributed to the medical staff for deciphering. Only one staff member among 58 respondents could interpret half of the items under survey; similarly, for 20 percent of the items listed, only half of the respondents were able to identify the meaning. Does "WNL" mean "Within Normal Limits," or "We Never Looked"!

TOPIC 14

Illegibility of Handwriting in Charts

Issue.   Illegibility of notes in medical records

Solution.   Short of grafting a typewriter onto each physician's writing arm or granting "CME credits for handwriting accomplishments," no simple remedy is obvious. Yet, individual instances of improvement have occurred: authorizing the use of a rubber signature stamp; mandating the use of typewritten histories and physicals; constructing a preprinted partially completed order form; constructing and using a partially completed history and physical examination checksheet; etc. One hospital simply shows a slide of the "worst handwriting of the week" at its weekly grand rounds, and presents an annual award to the notorious worst writer of the year.

Review Procedure
1. Obtain a sample of 50 charts of recently discharged hospitalized patients.
2. Appoint a review team of three individuals, including such possible participants as a nursing supervisor, a member of your medical auxiliary, a physician staff member, or a staff secretary.
3. Ask your medical records staff to flag a page of history and physical examination, a page of orders, and a page of consultation and ask each of the three members to review—separately—all (or specified) signatures for categorization as to *"easily legible," "questionably legible,"* or *"illegible."*

4. Tally the totals for each chart by each of the three committee members and then obtain the group totals.

5. The intended goal, of course, is to have none of the choices seen as illegible.

Actions To Be Taken

1. If all is in order, so notify the Medical Executive Committee and the medical staff at your next staff meeting.

2. If problems exist, consider possible solutions, choose one, implement it, re-audit the issue, and report to the Medical Executive Committee and the medical staff about the activity.

Added Point of Emphasis.   In one of Washington's hospitals, illegibility of signature was determined by the above method to exist in approximately 30 percent of the signatures on histories and physicians' orders and consultations. Illegibility on prescriptions necessitated an almost 20 percent "callback rate" to the writing physician and/or unit, wasting an enormous amount of time and costing the pharmacy, the physicians, and the hospital many dollars (not to mention angering multiple parties).

TOPIC 15

Terminating Life-Support Systems

Issue.   "Miscommunication" between patients, relatives, medical staffs, and hospital staffs regarding the termination of life-support procedures. Recent actions of the Washington State Supreme Court (*In re: Colyer* 1983) have provided guidelines about what ought to be done when confronted by this thorny problem.

Solution.   A previous risk management review unit (Topic 6) has addressed the question of "no code procedures." Similarly, the medical staff ought to document that the attending physician has discussed the issue of "terminating life-support measures" and has acted accordingly. The Washington State Supreme Court calls for a review by more than simply one attending physician (at least two others ought to be involved) and discussion of the matter with the patient and/or the relatives, as well as possible review by the courts.

Review Procedure

1. Obtain from Medical Records the charts of 30 patients who have recently expired in your hospital.

2. Review each case carefully to determine whether, in fact, any termination of life support took place—such data should be available in the progress notes, in the nurses' notes, on the order sheet, etc.

3. Should such terminations have taken place, review each record for the presence of documentation of appropriate consultations and notification of relatives.

4. Obtain copies of any medical staff minutes in the last two years which address this problem or any documentation of discussions of the matter by the Medical Executive Committee, and the development of a medical staff policy.

Actions To Be Taken

1. If all is in order, so notify your Medical Executive Committee and the medical staff at the next staff meeting.

2. If problems exist, devise a solution in cooperation with your hospital administrator, implement it, and re-audit the issue after approximately six months, reporting to the Medical Executive Committee and the medical staff about that activity.

Added Point of Emphasis. This particular issue—terminating life-support measures—is basic to the question posed in 1983 by the Reagan Administration with reference to "Baby Doe amendments" calling for federal intervention in the determination of life-support measures. Opponents of federal intervention have called for action on the local scene. Has your hospital or your medical staff taken any position or has it even discussed the matter?

Topic 16

Altered Records

Issue.   Altering medical records

Solution.   Eliminate the practice of "altering" (deceptively trying to change) as opposed to "correcting" records (entering additional or deleting incorrect information with appropriate notation of the date and author of the change).

Review Procedure

1. Obtain a sample of 50 medical records of recently discharged patients.

2. Appoint an ad hoc committee of one physician, one nurse, and one Medical Records Department staff member to review each medical record separately for (a) progress notes; (b) consultation reports; (c) order sheets; (d) operative reports (if present). Check for the presence of absence of entries which would appear to suggest to the reader an "altered" or incorrectly amended record. Tally the total number of items reviewed and the total number of possible "alterations" for each committee member and then tally the totals of the three members which are suggestive of alteration.

Actions To Be Taken

1. If all is in order, so notify the Medical Executive Committee and the medical staff at the next staff meeting.

2. If problems exist, attempt to devise a solution in your local hospital, implement it, re-audit the issue, and report to the Medical Executive Committee and the medical staff about both the activity and the outcome.

Added Point of Emphasis.   In Oregon, altered records have continued to cause significant losses with four large settlements being reached in the first six months of 1982, despite a major effort on the part of their Risk Management Program.

Topic 17

Recredentialing of Medical Staff

Issue.   Shortcomings in the original credentialing and particularly in the recredentialing of physician staff members

Solution.   Assure that each hospital's medical staff examines in detail both the operating plan for recredentialing its medical staff and what actually has been done for 30 most recently recredentialed physicians.

Review Procedure
1. Schedule an agenda item for an upcoming Medical Executive Committee meeting to compare the JCAH's recommendations regarding recredentialing with existent staff bylaws.
2. Regardless of the outcome of step 1, request your Executive Committee to select an ad hoc committee of three—a physician, a hospital administration representative, and a member of the board—to review the documentation supporting the recredentialing of the 30 most recently recredentialed staff members. Compare the results with the JCAH's recommended criteria as well as your staff bylaws.

Actions To Be Taken
1. Assure that the Executive Committee reviews the outcome of step 2 above and acts accordingly if change is called for.
2. Assure that the outcome of the review and its follow-up is reported to the medical staff.

Added Point of Emphasis.   Several physician-owned malpractice insurance companies have adopted a policy of mandating both a physical examination and a psychological examination of all physicians aged 65 and over—an action prompted by their individual and collective claims loss experience.

TOPIC 18

Date and Time of Orders

Issue.   Orders entered into the medical record inadequately dated or timed

Solution.   Assure that all orders entered into the medical record in your hospital have both the date and the time of day accompanying them.

Review Procedure

1. Obtain a sample of 50 records of recently discharged patients and analyze the first three orders entered in each for the presence or absence of the date and the hour of day.

2. Calculate the appropriate percentage for each category of those orders with and without dates and those with and without times.

Actions To Be Taken

1. If all is in order, so notify the Medical Executive Committee and the medical staff at the next staff meeting.

2. If problems exist, devise a solution, implement it, re-audit the issue, and report to the Medical Executive Committee and the medical staff.

Added Point of Emphasis.   In addition to establishing the precise date and timing of the entry so as to protect against liability, this arrangement is also especially helpful in periodically reviewing how long it actually takes for your patients to receive the treatments and/or medications you order.

TOPIC 19

Lawyers' Requests for Hospital Records

Issue. Releasing hospital records to an attorney without notifying the attending physician about the inquiry. More and more frequently lawyers are requesting records in instances involving potential litigation; the involved physician often learns of the request only after the plaintiff's suit has been filed.

Solution. Adopt the policy of joint notification of the hospital administrator (and/or his or her deputy), as well as the attending physician involved in the care of the patient about whom inquiries are made.

Review Procedure
1. With the cooperation of the hospital administration and the head of the Medical Records Department, review of the appropriate log of entries of legal inquiries for hospital records.

2. Review documentation in the involved charts—or in the log itself—indicating that the attending physician had been notified.

3. Regardless of existing documentation, contact a sample of the involved physicians to confirm that appropriate notification had actually been received.

Actions To Be Taken
1. If all is in order, so notify the Medical Executive Committee and the medical staff at the next staff meeting.

2. If problems exist, devise a solution, implement it, re-audit the issue, and report findings to the medical staff.

Added Point of Emphasis. According to data from some states, significant cooperation between hospital and involved physicians can take place in bringing about effective arrangements to assure that justice will be served. In other words, when either party—be it the physician or the hospital—learns of potential litigation, each should notify the other so that reasonable defense can be constructed.

Topic 20

Verbal Orders

Issue. Misunderstanding or misinterpreting verbal orders—including telephone orders

Solution. Determine what proportion of orders for patients in your hospital—*if any*—are verbal orders with subsequent discussion of the appropriateness of the circumstances surrounding their use. The only total protection is avoidance of verbal orders; since this is not a feasible goal, the frequency ought to be kept low and appropriate indications for the use of verbal orders ought to be identified and monitored.

Review Procedure
1. Obtain 50 charts for a sample of recently discharged patients, at least 10 of whom have spent time in intensive care, coronary care or the labor suite.
2. Review all the orders, tallying the total number of orders written—i.e., either individual or group entries to constitute the denominator and how many had been verbal orders to serve as the numerator.
3. Tally the totals in both groups and determine what percentage of the total orders were composed of verbal orders.
4. If the percentage exceeds 5 percent for the total sample, prepare a proposed listing of appropriate indications for the use of verbal orders and submit them to your Medical Executive Committee for their consideration.

Actions To Be Taken
1. If all is in order, so notify the Medical Executive Committee and the medical staff at the next staff meeting.
2. If a problem exists, devise the recommended list of appropriate indications for your Medical Executive Committee, bring it to them for their action, and, if implemented, re-audit the process six months hence.

Added Point of Emphasis.   One Washington hospital, priding itself on the accuracy, legibility, and completeness of its order sheets, was stunned to discover that approximately 14 percent of orders of non-intensive care medical patients were verbal orders. With so many similar-sounding names of medication, such practices are fraught with problems.

TOPIC 21

Second Visit to the Operating Room

Issue.   Patients who have had two or more visits to the operating room during a single admission

Solution.   Analyze the reasons underlying second visits to the operating room from a sample of patients admitted to your hospital for surgery.

Review Procedure
1. With the assistance of the operating room staff and the Medical Records Department, obtain a sample of charts of all patients who have experienced two or more surgeries during a single hospitalization over the past six months.
2. Separate those patients' charts wherein the second operation had been scheduled or planned at the time of admission from those where such planning had not occurred.
3. Review all remaining charts via your Quality Assurance Committee wherein no planned second surgery had been indicated at the time of admission. Consider the reasons underlying the second visit and the possibilities of avoiding those circumstances in the future.

Actions To Be Taken
1. If all is in order, so notify the Medical Executive Committee and the medical staff at the next staff meeting.
2. If problems exist, devise a solution, implement it, re-audit the

issue, and report to the Medical Executive Committee and the medical staff about that activity.

Added Point of Emphasis.   According to a review of malpractice cases closed in Washington since 1975, and quantified by the joint California Medical Association/California Hospital Association studies of malpractice in California, startlingly high numbers of malpractice cases have been associated with two or more visits to the operating room during a single admission. Particularly productive in the early detection of impending malpractice problems, a program of scanning discharges for those patients who have had second visits to operating rooms has been embodied in many "generic screening programs" now actively conducted in most progressive hospitals.

TOPIC 22

Anesthesiology Reports

Issue.   Contradictory statements appearing on anesthesiology records

Solution.   In all Washington hospital operating rooms the anesthesiologist is expected to complete an anesthesiology report with certain data being entered on a periodic basis. The necessity here is to assure that the data being entered in the anesthesiology report are concordant with other data being entered in the medical record and the operating room log.

Review Procedure
1. Obtain the medical records of 30 patients recently discharged from the hospital after an operating room event.
2. Secure a copy of the anesthesiology records from each of the medical records and, with the assistance of the medical records librarian, review each for the timing of the material included—such as the start of the operation, the termination of the operation, the timing of the administration of the blood, etc.

3. Carefully review other possible details, such as the signature of more than one anesthesiologist, the comments of the circulating nurse, and the timing mentioned in the operating room log, to assure that there are no discrepancies.

Actions To Be Taken

1. If all is in order, so notify your Medical Executive Committee and the medical staff at the next staff meeting.

2. If problems exist, devise a solution in cooperation with your hospital administrator, implement it, and re-audit the issue after approximately six months, reporting to the Medical Executive Committee and the medical staff about that activity.

Added Point of Emphasis. Two Washington anesthesiologists have recently reviewed all of the malpractice cases against anesthesiologists for the past decade; they were astounded to learn of some of the deficiencies which appeared repeatedly, such as the absence of the anesthesiologist from the operating room while the patient was under general anesthesia. All in all, a simple review of anesthesiology records could assure each hospital that it is in full compliance with existing recommendations.

TOPIC 23

Telephone Messages

Issue. Failure to document messages transmitted by telephone or in person

Solution. In all of our hospitals and our offices, assure that appropriate documentation of telephone messages is completed in a retrievable fashion.

Review Procedure. With the assistance of your hospital administrator, the director of nursing, and the director of your Medical Records Department, determine if any policies have been developed or implemented regarding documentation of telephone conversations, e.g.:

1. If the laboratory calls a test result to the patient care unit, who is authorized to record that result? Does the laboratory later validate the accuracy of the documentation?

2. If an attorney contacts the hospital regarding a patient, who is authorized to document the details of the conversation and who, if anyone, reviews such documentation?

3. If a relative is called regarding a probable discharge time of a patient, is that telephone call documented anywhere?

4. If a consent to an operative procedure needs to be obtained by telephone, who documents that such had, in fact, been obtained?

5. If a patient dies unexpectedly and the family is told by phone about the event, who—if anyone—documents the conversation and its timing?

Actions To Be Taken

1. If all seems to be in order, so notify your Medical Executive Committee and the medical staff at the next staff meeting.

2. If problems exist, devise a solution in cooperation with your hospital administrator, implement it, and re-audit the issue after approximately six months, reporting to the Medical Executive Committee and the medical staff about that activity.

Added Point of Emphasis.   Little doubt exists that communication failures underlie the lion's share of malpractice actions in the state of Washington. The physician who documents communications will find himself/herself in a far better position to defend against such allegations in the future.

Topic 24

Incident Report Follow-ups

Issue.   Failure of hospitals and their medical staffs to follow up on "deficiencies" detected in incident reports

Solution. Incident reports are filed, in Washington hospitals, by nursing and/or other hospital staff employees concerning those situations which may result in an allegation of malpractice against either the hospital or its medical staff members. It is expected that when such reports are filed in line with Quality Assurance Committee activities, they will be "privileged" communications—but, nevertheless, this question of confidentiality remains at issue. Regardless, it is mandatory that appropriate responses to detected deficiencies be demonstrated and implemented.

Review Procedure

1. Obtain the cooperation of your hospital administrator, and, with the assistance of the medical records librarian and two physicians, review the recent follow-up of 20 incident reports received by hospital administration during the prior six months, but none more recently than two months ago.

2. Each follow-up ought to contain a statement regarding the documentation of the perceived deficit, corrective actions which have been or will be implemented, and a reporting period at the end of which an assessment of the correction of the situation will be made.

Actions To Be Taken

1. If all is in order, so notify your Medical Executive Committee and the medical staff at the next staff meeting.

2. If problems exist, devise a solution in cooperation with your hospital administrator, implement it, and re-audit the issue after approximately six months, reporting to the Medical Executive Committee and the medical staff about that activity.

Added Point of Emphasis. While some debate continues in Washington regarding the "confidentiality" of incident reports, no debate would seem to be possible regarding the responsibility of the "corporate hospital" (including the corporate medical staff) to act on detected deficiencies in a responsible professional manner. Moreover, the Washington State Supreme Court has now ruled that appropriately appointed peer review committee deliberations and conclusions are immune from "discovery."

Topic 25

Outside Laboratory Reports

Issue.   Failure of attending physicians to determine what has been reported to their hospitals by outside laboratories

Solution.   In all hospitals, as well as in all physician offices, assure that any and all outside laboratory reports are carefully reviewed before filing.

Review Procedure

1. With the cooperation of your clinical laboratory (or clinical pathology) director, obtain a listing of 30 patients who had laboratory tests, other than PKU, performed outside the hospital's premises (i.e., sent to another laboratory); obtain the number of the chart and, from it, the name of the physician involved.

2. Have the Medical Records Department pull each of the charts to determine if the laboratory result has been returned to the hospital and documented in the chart. Verify your findings via the laboratory's log.

3. Contact the attending physician and/or his or her office to ascertain whether he or she had actually learned of the results; determine how the information was transmitted.

Actions To Be Taken

1. If all seems to be in order, so notify your Medical Executive Committee and the medical staff at the next staff meeting.

2. If problems exist, devise a solution in cooperation with your hospital administrator, implement it, and re-audit the issue after approximately six months, reporting to the Medical Executive Committee and the medical staff about that activity.

Added Point of Emphasis.   In Washington, several sizeable awards have resulted from the "failure to notice" abnormal laboratory results—some of which were filed in charts without having been scrutinized by the responsible physician. In one instance a $1.1 million award resulted.

Topic 26
Circumcision

Issue. Circumcising a baby when the parents did not want the procedure carried out or failing to circumcise after the parents have requested circumcision. Part of the problem is communication: Who discusses the procedure with the parents?

Solution. In all hospitals, the physician responsible should be the party to discuss the pros and cons of circumcision with the parents and to document the informed consent.

Review Procedure
1. Obtain the records of 30 recently discharged male infants who were circumcised at your hospital.
2. Review each chart to determine the presence of an informed consent and appraise the adequacy of its completion.
3. Contact each responsible physician by phone or in person to ask if he or she specifically recalls discussing the matter of the pros and cons with the parents.
4. Ask the nursery or obstetrical suite supervisor for his or her opinion about the traditional practices on the local scene.

Actions To Be Taken
1. If all is in order, so notify your Medical Executive Committee and the medical staff at the next staff meeting.
2. If problems exist, devise a solution in cooperation with your hospital administrator, implement it, and re-audit the issue after approximately six months, reporting to the Medical Executive Committee and the medical staff about that activity.

Added Point of Emphasis. In a recent release from the American College of Surgeons, it is of interest to note that among the 10 most frequently performed surgical procedures, circumcision is not even mentioned, although it is most common! It is totally ignored. Unfortunately, ignoring the issue has led to one successful suit in Washington State in excess of $350,000.

Topic 27

Hospital Discharge Instructions

Issue.   Failure to document instructions being given to patients at the time of their discharge from the hospital

Solution.   Assure that 100 percent of charts document that matters of import to the patient have been discussed with him or her prior to discharge.

Review Procedure

1. Obtain a sample of 30 charts of patients recently discharged from your hospital.

2. Examine each chart for the presence of any documentation that the following items were discussed with the patient: (a) treatment measures, if any; (b) activity limitations, if any; (c) drugs prescribed, if any; (d) location of scheduled follow-up, if any; (e) time of scheduled follow-up, if any.

Actions To Be Taken

1. If all is in order, so notify your Medical Executive Committee and the medical staff at the next staff meeting.

2. If problems exist, devise a solution in cooperation with your hospital administrator, implement it, and re-audit the issue after approximately six months, reporting to the Medical Executive Committee and the medical staff about that activity.

Added Point of Emphasis.   In many hospitals a "discharge planning" procedure has been put into effect which checks the nursing staff record to see whether, in fact, adequate information has been transmitted to the patient. Do you have any analogous procedure in your hospital?

Topic 28

Fetal Monitoring

Issue.   Monitoring of the labor process—with particular reference to "fetal monitoring"

Solution.   In all hospitals, assure that the issue of fetal monitoring has received appropriate discussion among the medical staff and that appropriate policies have been adopted for implementation in the labor suite.

Review Procedure
1. Meet with the chief of Obstetrics in departmentalized hospitals or the appropriate party in nondepartmentalized hospitals to determine if any official discussion has been recorded in staff minutes as having taken place regarding fetal monitoring, its indications, the equipment necessary, and the review processes to be involved.
2. Ask the individual physician about his/her perception of the satisfactoriness of the overall fetal monitoring process. Is it able to be instituted rapidly, does the equipment work, is the staff acquainted with interpretations, etc.?
3. Meet with the obstetrical suite supervisor to determine his/her perception of any policies or usual practices regarding the medical staff's indications for and use of fetal monitoring. In other words, do such practices actually exist?
4. Ask the obstetrical supervisor to comment on his/her staff's perception of the satisfactoriness of the equipment's performance and the appropriateness of the use of the equipment in view of step 3.
5. Determine from your hospital administration if any incident reports have been filed regarding the issue of fetal monitoring and, if so, what (if any) steps were taken to remedy the perceived problem.

Actions To Be Taken
1. If all seems to be in order, so notify your Medical Executive Committee and the medical staff at the next staff meeting.

2. If problems exist, devise a solution in cooperation with your hospital administrator, implement it, and re-audit the issue after approximately six months, reporting to the Medical Executive Committee and the medical staff about that activity.

Added Point of Emphasis.　Both in the State of Washington and on the national scene, "damaged baby" cases account for enormous malpractice awards. Quite obviously, the expenses for a 70-year life expectancy of a damaged infant are enormous. Only by avoiding as many as possible of such detrimental consequences, or by not being liable for having failed to try to avoid them, can we look toward the reduction of this significant cost—and the betterment of patient care.

Topic 29

Information Sources

Issue.　Failure to obtain precise information about a drug or a procedure, and then act on it

Solution.　Assure that a process is in place to provide (or arrange to provide) answers to questions posed by physicians where specific answers are currently available.

Review Procedure
1. Meet with the individual in charge of the medical library.
2. Pose five specific questions to that individual such as the following:
   (a) What are the teratogenic effects of dicoumeral?
   (b) What are the renal contraindications to using Gentamicin?
   (c) What are the current reporting requirements re: scarlet fever?
   (d) Where and when is the 1985 annual meeting of the WSMA?
   (e) What are the current recommendations regarding immunization versus antibody administration for management of suspected rabies infections?

3. Ask your medical library's representative to estimate how much time, for non-emergency problems, it would take to obtain the answers to the five questions.

4. After that estimated time interval has elapsed, check back with the medical library representative to determine if the answers had been obtained—and whether they are accurate.

Actions To Be Taken

1. If all seems to be in order, so notify your Medical Executive Committee and the medical staff at the next staff meeting.

2. If problems exist, devise a solution in cooperation with your hospital administrator, implement it, and re-audit the issue after approximately six months, report to the Medical Executive Committee and the medical staff about that activity.

Added Point of Emphasis.   Quite obviously, no hospital and no one library can store all the information necessary to carry on today's modern medical practice. But, with the use of the telephone, answers can be sought—for those who are tuned in to asking the appropriate questions. In Washington State, three physicians were recently each found negligent for having failed to conduct a literature review about the potential effects of a drug on a patient—and the cost of that negligence has been set at $6.4 million!

TOPIC 30

Consultation Notes

Issue.   Failure of the consultation process

Solution.   In all hospitals, and also in all physicians' offices, the consultation process ought to be carried out in line with professional standards and expectations.

Review Procedure.   Obtain the assistance of the Medical Records Department to identify 30 charts of patients recently discharged from the hospital who had consultations performed during hospitalization. Review each chart to assess the following factors:

1. Is the mechanism for obtaining the consultation recorded; i.e., was a telephone call made, an order written, or a "consultation form" completed?

2. Is there any documentation of the specific questions posed to the consultant?

3. Is there documentation of the time lapse between the request for the consultation and its completion by the consultant? If there is such documentation, does the time lapse seem "reasonable"?

4. Were the recommendations of the consultant addressed by the attending physician—i.e., were any resulting orders initiated, was the patient transferred to another service, etc.?

5. On a scale of 1 (bad) to 10 (outstanding) was the specific consultative process completed in a "proper professional manner"?

After the review of 30 such consultations and the assignment of an appropriate rating to each, add the total numbers, divide by 30, and obtain the average numerical rating for initiating the consultation process in your hospital.

Actions To Be Taken

1. If all seems to be in order, so notify your Medical Executive Committee and the medical staff at the next staff meeting.

2. If problems exist, devise a solution in cooperation with your hospital administrator, implement it, and re-audit the issue after approximately six months, reporting to the Medical Executive Committee and the medical staff about that activity.

Added Point of Emphasis. Proper consultation is the backbone of modern medical practice. On a number of occasions, associated disputes entered in the medical record have "spoken for themselves" in finalizing the jury's assessment of malpractice. In Washington's hospitals, it is appropriate to record differences of opinions but in such a fashion as not to add gasoline to the existing malpractice inferno.

Index

209